MOTIVATION PSYCHOLOGY

GET OFF YOUR BUTT NOW!

Light That Fire Under Your Ass And Start Cracking Big Time!

Troy Ball

Table of Contents

Chapter 1: How To Succeed In Life 6
Chapter 2: How Do You Make Working Enjoyable 10
Chapter 3: Overcoming Fear and Self-Doubt 16
Chapter 4: Meditate For Focus 19
Chapter 5: How to Learn Faster 22
Chapter 6: How To Use Affirmations For Success 25
Chapter 7: It's Okay To Feel Uncertain 27
Chapter 8: *The Daily Routine Experts for Peak Productivity* 30
Chapter 9: Gravitational Leadership 33
Chapter 10: Fight Lethargy and Win 35
Chapter 11: How Distraction Robs You of Joy 39
Chapter 12: Playing To Your Strengths 42
Chapter 13: The Power of Developing Eye Contact with Your Client 46
Chapter 14: *The Goal Is Not The Point* 49
Chapter 15: Creating Successful Habits 52
Chapter 16: *8 Ways On How To Start Taking Actions* 56
Chapter 17: Why You've Come Too Far To Quit 61
Chapter 18: Becoming High Achievers 65
Chapter 19: 5 Ways To Deal with Personal Feelings of Inferiority 69
Chapter 20: Being Open To Opportunities For Social Events 72
Chapter 21: Develop A Habit of Studying 76
Chapter 22: 8 Common Mistakes That Cause You to Make Bad Decisions 79
Chapter 23: *Be Motivated by Challenge* 84
Chapter 24: Don't Wait Another Second To Live Your Dreams 87
Chapter 25: Do The Painful Things First 91
Chapter 26: 7 Ways To Know If You're A Good Person 93
Chapter 27: Stay Focused 98

Chapter 28: How To Start Working Immediately 103

Chapter 29: How to Love Yourself First 107

Chapter 30: Why You're Demotivated By A Values Conflict 110

Chapter 31: Why Are You Working So Hard 113

Chapter 32: Don't Make Life Harder Than It Needs To Be 117

Chapter 33: 6 Ways To Get Full Attention From People Around You
.... 121

Chapter 34: 7 Ways On How To Expect Change For The Better In Your Life 126

Chapter 1:
How To Succeed In Life

"You can't climb the ladder of success with your hands in your pocket."

Every day that you're living, make a habit of making the most out of it. Make a habit of winning today. Don't dwell on the past, don't worry about the future. You just have to make sure that you're winning today. Move a little forward every day; take a little step every day. And when you're giving your fruitful efforts, you're making sure you're achieving your day, then you start to built confidence within yourselves. Confidence is when you close your eyes at night and see a vision, a dream, a goal, and you believe that you're going to achieve it. When you're doing things, when you're productive the whole day, then that long journey will become short in a matter of time.

Make yourself a power list for each day. Take a sheet of paper, write Monday on top of it and then write five critical, productive, actionable tasks that you're going to do that day. After doing the task, cross it off. Repeat the process every day of every week of every month till you get closer to achieving your goals, your dreams. It doesn't matter if you're doing the same tasks every day or how minor or major they are; what matters is that it's creating momentum in things that you've believed you couldn't do. And as soon as the momentum gets completed, you start to believe that you can do something. You eventually stop writing your tasks down because now they've become your new habits. You need a reminder for them. You don't need to cross them off because you're going to do them. The power list helps you win the day. You're stepping out of your comfort zone, doing something that looks uncomfortable for starters, but while doing this, even for a year, you will see yourself standing five years from where you're standing today.

Decide, commit, act, succeed, repeat. If you want to be an inspiration to others, a motivator to others, impact others somehow, you have to self-evaluate certain perceptions and think that'll help you change the way you see yourself and the world. Perseverance, hard-working, and consistency would be the keywords if one were to achieve success in life. You just have to keep yourself focused on your ultimate goal. You will fall a hundred times. There's always stumbling on the way. But if you have the skill, the power, the instinct to get yourself back up every time you fall, and to dig yourself out of the whole, then no one can stop you. You have to control the situation, Don't ever let the situation control you. You're living life exactly as it should be. If you don't like what you're living in, then consider changing the aspects. The person you are right now versus the person you want to be in the future, there's only a fine line between the two that you have to come face-to-face with.

Your creativity is at most powerful the moment you open your eyes and start your day. That's when you get the opportunity to steer your emotions and thoughts in the direction that you want them to go, not the other way around. Every failure is a step closer to success. We won't succeed on the first try, and we will never have it perfect by trying it only once. But we can master the art of not giving up. We dare to take risks. If we never fail, we never get the chance of getting something we never had. We can never taste the fruits of success without falling. The difference between successful people and those who aren't successful is the point of giving up.

Success isn't about perfection. Instead, it's about getting out of bed each day, clearing the dust off you, and thinking like a champion, a winner, going on about your day, being productive, and making the most out of it. Remember that the mind controls your body; your body doesn't hold your mind. You have to make yourself mentally tough to overcome the fears and challenges that come in the way of your goals. As soon as you get up in the morning, start thinking about anything or anyone that you're grateful for. Your focus should be on making yourself feel good and confident enough to get yourself through the day.

The negative emotions that we experience, like pain or rejection, or frustration, cannot always make our lives miserable. Instead, we can consider them as our most incredible friends that'll drive us to success. When people succeed, they tend to party. When they fail, they tend to ponder. And the pondering helps us get the most victories in our lives. You're here, into another day, still breathing fine, that means you got another chance, to better yourself, to be able to right your wrongs. Everyone has a more significant potential than the roles they put themselves in.

Trust yourself always. Trust your instinct—no matter what or how anyone thinks. You're perfectly capable of doing things your way. Even if they go wrong, you always learn something from them. Don't ever listen to the naysayers. You've probably heard a million times that you can't do this and you can't do that, or it's never even been done before. So what? So what if no one has ever done it before. That's more of the reason for you to do it since you'll become the first person to do it. Change that 'You can't' into 'Yes, I definitely can.' Muhammad Ali, one of the greatest boxers to walk on the face of this planet, was once asked, 'how many sit-ups do you do?' to which he replied, 'I don't count my sit-ups. I only start counting when it starts hurting. When I feel pain, that's when I start counting because that's when it really counts.' So we get a wonderful lesson to work tirelessly and shamelessly if we were to achieve our dreams. Dr. Arnold Schwarzenegger beautifully summed up life's successes in 6 simple rules; Trust yourself, Break some rules, Don't be afraid to fail, Ignore the naysayers, Work like hell, And give something back.

Chapter 2:
How Do You Make Working Enjoyable

In today's topic, we are going to talk about something that I think everybody would wish in their work today, to enjoy their jobs and not see it as a means to an end but something fun and exciting.

That they are able to get up every single morning with love that their is going to be spent on something fun that happens to make them money, rather than waking up feeling dread that they have to trade their hours in exchange for a paycheck.

For me personally, there's no worse feeling than waking from a peaceful slumber after a good night's rest only to feel your heart sink as you realize that you are are about to go into a day doing something that you are just not at all excited about to do. That the work has just become either really stale, stressful, or pointless. That maybe, on some level, you have nothing more to give in your current job, and you are just going through the motions without much thought or control over your future.

Before we go into quick fixes on how we can possibly change our work environment to make it more enjoyable through sheer force and willpower. Let us look at some of the ways that work was fun without us even having to try.

I believe that one of few times in our lives that work was enjoyable is usually when we start in a new job, or begin a new career path. During the initial stages of your new job, you are constantly learning new things, constantly growing, constantly acquiring new knowledge… That constant drive to learn gives us something to look forward to each day, that we do not really know what to expect, and that feeling is exciting. We are meeting new colleagues, establishing new connections, and growing our network. How many of you will agree with me that this is truly a fun and exciting period of time?

After a while when things start to become stable, when your job starts to become predictable, and things start to turn stale, we in fact lose that enjoyment that we once had despite the pay being higher than when we first began our job. So really if you look at it, money isn't the sole motivator of what makes work enjoyable, but rather growth, and learning new things. As with everything including humans, if we don't grow, we are essentially dying. And if we do not feed our soul with things that move us forward, we are in fact marching towards "death". And that decline leads us to feeling that we do not derive the same enjoyment as we once had. In this instance, one might consider pursuing a new career path or picking up a new skill to feed that constant hunger for growth.

A second way that makes work enjoyable is really simple, and it is that you really do love what you do. And you do not mind spending hours on end working hard on the job because it simply isn't all that hard to do. Look at the very successful entrepreneurs of today's world, they absolutely love what they do and they have no problems dedicating their whole lives to their mission despite having billions of dollars at their disposal. They work not because they need the money, which they obviously do not, they work because that want to. And in order for us to find that, we really have to be willing to let go of our current jobs, no matter how high paying and secure they are, in search of that thing that fills us to the very core. Now i am not encouraging u all to simply quit your jobs because there are practical concerns to be had, such as commitments you might have, like paying down your house loan, expenses in raising your children, college funds, car payments etc. In that instance I would encourage you to think hard about what is the next best step after you have settled all these financial commitments, because there could be a possibility that your calling may not end up paying you that well. You will have to then consider whether it is worth sacrificing that high pay for something that calls to your soul. That is a choice that you will have to make for yourself.

Another natural way that one might feel that work is enjoyable is the company that they surround themselves with. And by company, I mean colleagues. Personally, i do feel that colleagues play a huge role in the way that one might derive enjoyment from their work. Because having colleagues that you really like to work with on a daily basis, can make or break your time at your job. When you have good colleagues, you have an outlet to vent frustrations, bounce ideas off one another, and build a social support group of sorts that will help pull u through the toughest of challenges that you might face in the company. It is tough going through the wilderness alone. Life is always better with other people in the party. And you will notice that once those colleagues starts leaving the company, for whatever reason, that there are lesser and lesser reasons for you personally to stay in the company yourself. Take a look back at your previous jobs where you are one of the last few left and tell me whether that is true. It is as if your pack has left, and that magnetic pull that has kept you in the company for that long no longer has that attraction power left anymore.

For those who are working alone, or remotely from home, I share your pain in not having colleagues next to you or around you to talk to. And being an entrepreneur can sometimes be an isolating or lonely business. And there are many times when I myself have thought of giving up because it just because too excruciatingly lonely. But for those who are on the same boat as me, I have a solution for you which has worked for me personally. And that is to consider a co-working space if that option is available to you. For me, a co-working space has worked wonders in bringing in the social aspect back into my work life. You realize that when you are working in such a space, that there are like-minded individuals who are also on the same boat as you. There you might get the motivation you need to stay on your unique path and you can even get to opportunity to make friends there as well. I believe that isolating yourself at home, whilst it might save you money, is not very healthy mentally and emotionally in the long run. We are not meant to always be at home without interacting with other human beings. We are social creatures after all and we need to fill that tank in order to feel happy and connected with the world outside.

Now we will bring ourselves back to those who are working in a regular 9-5 job, which is probably the majority of you guys. This next one might not be within your control, as is the case with your colleagues leaving, but I do believe the next factor that would make or break an enjoyable working experience would be the culture and business philosophy of the company. Is your company one that encourages fresh new ideas? Or one that promotes and enforces a system of hierarchy and chain of commands? Where approval of a new idea has to move up a chain before it gets reviewed and accepted? Does the company promote freely sharing knowledge and wisdom with a good work life balance? Or one that stifles creativity and overworks their employees to milk every last dollar for the company's bottom line? I am sure you know exactly what your company's culture is like. But the question is whether on any level do you accept it as a fact or are doing anything about it to change your work environment. It is in my personal opinion, that the best companies to work for, and the best employers to work for, are ones that foster creativity and personal growth for their employees. That one should be allowed to express their ideas freely and to be themselves as much as is within the proper boundaries of a workplace environment. If you feel that you are currently not in that particular place, well u should definitely consider doing something about it for sure.

Finally, we shall move on to what you can actually do that is within your control to maximize your enjoyment of a typical workday, putting aside all the factors that we have discussed prior. I think the simplest way that you start to tweak is to change little things in your workstation. If your desk has too much stuff all over the place, you might consider tidying it up nicely and decluttering your space to make it more aesthetically pleasing. Clutter has the unwanted effect of making us feel like everything is out of place which could translate it to our own productivity workflow as well. Next you might consider getting an ergonomic chair that makes you feel well supported when you sit on it. Next you can consider the 5 minute rule, if you haven't seen that video, click on the link above to go watch it. It might be the solution that you have been searching for. Finally, set rewards that would motivate you to begin work. For example for every hour that you work, you get to reward yourself with a treat, whether it be a snack, a cup of your favorite tea or coffee, or even a quick 5-10minute video. But do not wander off for too long otherwise you might break the flow of productivity and it would be less enjoyable if you have to force yourself back into work mode again.

Chapter 3:
Overcoming Fear and Self-Doubt

The lack of belief most people have is the reason for their failure at even the smallest things in life. The biggest killer of dreams is the lack of belief in ourselves and the doubt of failure.

We all make mistakes. We all have some ghosts of the past that haunt us. We all have something to hide. We all have something that we regret. But what you are today is not the result of your mistakes.

You are here because of your struggles to make those things go away. You are here now with the power and strength to shape your present and your future.

Our mind is designed to take the shape of what we hold long enough inside it. The things we frequently think about ultimately start filling in the spaces within our memory, so we have to be careful. We have to decide whether we want to stay happy or to hold on to the fear we once wanted to get rid of.

The human spirit and human soul are colored by the impressions we ourselves decide to impose.

The reason why we don't want to explore the possibility of what to do is that subconsciously we don't believe that it can happen for us. We don't believe that we deserve it or if it was meant for us.

So here is something I suggest. Ask yourself, how much time in a day do you spend thinking about your dream? How much time do you spend working on your dreams everyday? What books did you read this year? What new skills have you acquired recently? What have you done that makes you worthy of your dream? Nothing?

Then you are on point with your doubt because you don't have anything to show for when the opportunity presents itself.

You don't succeed because you have this latent fear. Fear that makes you think about the consequences of what will happen if you fail even with all the good things on your hand?

I know that feeling but failure is there to teach you one important and maybe the most essential skill life can teach us; Resilience.

You rediscover your life once you have the strength to fight your every fear and every doubt because you have better things on your hand to care for.

You have another dream to pursue. Another horizon awaits you. Another peak to summit. It doesn't matter if you literally have to run to stand still. You got to do what you got to do, no matter the consequences and the sacrifices.

But failing to do what is required of you has no justifiable defense. Not even fear. Because your fears are self-imposed and you already have many wrong things going on for you right now.

Don't let fear be one of them. Because fear is the most subtle and destructive disease So inhale all your positive energies and exhale all your doubts because you certainly are a better person without them.

Chapter 4:
Meditate For Focus

Meditation calms the mind and helps you to focus on what is important. It dims the noise and brings your goals into clearer vision.

Meditation has been practised as far back as 5000bc in India - with meditation depicted in wall artisan from that period.
That is 1500 years older than any written artefact ever found.
It is as old as the archaeological evidence of any human society.

Meditation can change the structure of the brain promoting focus, learning and better memory, as well as lowering stress and reducing the chances of anxiety and depression.

Whilst there are many different types and ways to meditate,
the ultimate goal is to clear your mind and calm your body
so that you can focus on your dream.
Aim to look inward for answers.
It could be aided by music relating to your dream or videos.
The music, the images, and imagining you are already living that life will bring it into reality.

Your mind creates the vision and the feeling
in your heart will bring it to you.

When your mind and heart work together it creates balance,
leading to happiness and success.

Meditation is the process of bringing the
visions of the mind and the desires of the heart together,
which in turn will form your life.
Meditation clears all the threats to this -
such as worry and distraction.
It will bring you clear focus and open up the next steps in your journey.

Meditation is often best done when you first wake or before you go to
sleep, but it can be incorporated into your day.
If clear consistent thought brings decisive action and success,
it is important to dwell on your dreams as often as possible.
Calm your mind of the unnecessary noise that is robbing you of your
focus.

The more realistic you make this vision
and the more you feel it in your heart,
the quicker it will come.

Meditation can help you achieve this
whether you follow a guide or make it up yourself.
The key is calm and focus.

Your subconscious knows how to get there.
Meditation will help open up that knowledge.

Science is just beginning to unlock the answers on why meditation is so effective, even so it has been used for over 7000 years to help people relax and focus on their goals.

The positive health and well-being evidence of meditation is well documented.
We may not yet understand it fully,
But just know that it works and use it every day.
You don't need to understand every detail to use something that works.
Meditation is perhaps one of the most time tested tools in existence.
It could work for you, if you try it.
It could change your life forever.

Chapter 5:
How to Learn Faster

Remember the saying, "You are never too old to learn something new"? Believe me, it's not true in any way you understood it.

The most reliable time to learn something new was the time when you were growing up. That was the time when your brain was in its most hyperactive state and could absorb anything you had thrown at it.

You can still learn, but you would have to change your approach to learning.

You won't learn everything, because you don't like everything going on around you. You naturally have an ego to please. So what can you do to boost your learning? Let's simplify the process. When you decide to learn something, take a moment and ask yourself this; "Will this thing make my life better? Will this fulfill my dreams? Will I benefit from it?".

If you can answer all these questions in a positive, you will pounce on the thing and you won't find anyone more motivated than you.

Learning is your brain's capability to process things constructively. If you pick up a career, you won't find it hard to flourish if you are genuinely interested in that particular skill.

Whether it be sports, singing, entrepreneurship, cooking, writing, or anything you want to pursue. Just ask yourself, can you use it to increase your creativity, your passion, your satisfaction. If you can, you will start learning it as if you knew it all along.

Your next step to learning faster would be to improve and excel at what you already have. How can you do that? It's simple yet again!

Ask yourself another question, that; "Why must I do this? Why do I need this?" if you get to answer that, you will find the fastest and effective way to the top yourself without any coaching. Why will this happen on its own? Because now you have found a purpose for your craft and the destination is clear as the bright sun in the sky.

The last but the most important thing to have a head start on your journey of learning is the simplest of them all, but the hardest to opt for. The most important step is to start working towards things.

The flow of learning is from Head to Heart to Hands. You have thought of the things you want to do in your brain. Then you asked your heart if it satisfied you. Now it's time to put your hands to work.

You never learn until you get the chance to experience the world yourself. When you go through a certain event, your brain starts to process the outcomes that could have been, and your heart tells you to give it one more try. Here is the deciding moment. If you listen to your heart right away, you will get on a path of learning that you have never seen before.

What remains now is your will to do what you have decided. And when you get going, you will find the most useful resources immediately. Use your instincts and capitalize your time. Capture every chance with sheer will and belief as if this is your final moment for your dreams to come true.

It doesn't matter if you are not the ace in the pack, it doesn't matter if you are not in your peak physical shape, it doesn't matter if you don't have the money yet. You will someday get all those things only if you had the right skills and the right moment.

For all you know, this moment right now is the most worth it moment. So don't go fishing in other tanks when you have your own aquarium. That aquarium is your body, mind, and soul. All you need is to dive deep with sheer determination and the stars are your limit.

Chapter 6:
How To Use Affirmations For Success

Affirmations are best described as a self-help strategy that is used to promote self-confidence and belief in your abilities. There might come a million instances where you felt like you needed to affirm yourself, and there would be many moments when you have probably affirmed yourself without even realizing it. Simple sentences like "I've got what it takes" or "I believe in my ability to succeed" shift your focus away from the perceived inadequacies or failures and direct your focus towards your strengths. While affirmations may not be a magic bullet for instant success, they generally work as a tool for shifting your mindset and achieving your goals.

Neuroplasticity, or our brain's ability to adapt and change to different circumstances throughout our lives, makes us understand what makes affirmations work and how to make them more effective. Creating a mental image beforehand of doing something that you're scared of, like acing a nerve-wracking interview or bungee jumping to conquer your fear of heights, can encourage your brain to take these positive affirmations as fact, and soon your actions will tend to follow.

Repeating affirmations can help you boost your confidence and motivation, but you still must take some action yourself. Affirmations are a step towards the change, not the change itself. They can also help you to achieve your goals by strengthening your confidence by reminding you that you're in control of your success and what you can do right now to achieve it. Affirmations give you a list of long-standing patterns and beliefs, and it makes you act as if you've already succeeded. Understand that affirmations alone can't produce a change in every situation. You have to take some actions too along with them. Similarly, affirming your traits can also help you see yourself in a new light.

To get the most benefits from affirmations, start a regular practice and make it a habit. Say affirmations upon waking up and getting into bed; give them at least 3-5 minutes. Repeat each of your affirmations ten times, focus on the words that leave your mouth. Believe them to be true while saying them. Make it a consistent habit. You have to be patient and stick with your practice, and it might take some time before you see evident changes. Practicing affirmations can also activate the reward system in your brain, which can impact how you experience both emotional and physical pain. The moment you start managing your stress and other life difficulties, it would help you promote faith in yourself and boost self-empowerment.

Chapter 7:
It's Okay To Feel Uncertain

We are surrounded by a world that has endless possibilities. A world where no two incidents can predict the other. A realm where we are a slave to the unpredictable future and its repercussions.

Everyone has things weighing on their mind. Some of us know it and some of us keep carrying these weights unknowingly.

The uncertainty of life is the best gift that you never wanted. But when you come to realize the opportunities that lie at every uneven corner are worth living for.

Life changes fast, sometimes in our favor and sometimes not much. But life always has a way to balance things out. We only need to find the right approach to make things easier for us and the ones around us.

Everyone gets tested once in a while, but we need to find ways to cope with life when things get messy.

The worst thing the uncertainty of life can produce is the fear in your heart. The fear to never know what to expect next. But you can never let fear rule you.

To worry about the future ahead of us is pointless. So change the question from 'What if?' to 'What will I do if.'

If you already have this question popping up in your brain, this means that you are already getting the steam off.

You don't need to fear the uncertain because you can never wreck your life in any such direction from where there is no way back.

The uncertainty of life is always a transformation period to make you realize your true path. These uncertainties make you realize the faults you might have in your approach to things.

You don't need to worry about anything unpredictable and unexpected because not everything is out of your control every time. Things might not happen in a way you anticipated but that doesn't mean you cannot be prepared for it.

There are a lot of things that are in your control and you are well researched and well equipped to go around events. So use your experience to do the damage control.

Let's say you have a pandemic at your hand which you couldn't possibly predict, but that doesn't mean you cannot do anything to work on its effects. You can raise funds for the affected population. You can try to find new ways to minimize unemployment. You can find alternate ways to keep the economy running and so on.

Deal with your emotions as you cannot get carried away with such events being driven by your feelings.

Don't avoid your responsibilities and don't delay anything. You have to fulfill every task expected of you because you were destined to do it. The results are not predetermined on a slate but you can always hope for the best be the best version of yourself no matter how bad things get.

Life provides us with endless possibilities because when nothing is certain, anything is possible. So be your own limit.

Chapter 8:
The Daily Routine Experts for Peak Productivity

What is the one thing we want to get done for a successful life? That is an effective daily routine to go through the day, every day. History is presented as an example that every high achiever has had a good routine for their day. Some simple changes in our life can change the outcome drastically. We have to take the experts' advice for a good lifestyle. We have to choose everything, from color to college, ourselves. But an expert's advice gives us confidence in our choice.

You have to set the bar high so that you get your product at the end of the day. Experts got their peak productivity by shaping their routine in such a way that it satisfies them. The productivity expert Tim Ferriss gave us a piece of simple yet effective advice for such an outcome. He taught us the importance of controlling oneself and how essential it is to provide yourself with a non-reactive practice. When you know how to control yourself, life gets more manageable, as it gives you the power to prevent many things. It reduces stress which gets your productivity out.

Another productive expert of ours, Cal Newport, gives us his share of information. He is always advising people to push themselves to their limits. He got successful by giving his deep work more priority than other work. He is managing multitasks at the same time while being a husband and a father. He is a true example of a good routine that leads to positive productivity. It would help if you decided what matters to you the most and need to focus on that. Get your priorities straight and work toward those goals. Construct your goals and have a clear idea of what your next step will be. It will result in increasing your confidence.

Now, the questions linger that how to start your day? Early is the answer. Early to bed and early to rising has been the motto of productive people. As Dan Ariely said, there is a must 3 hours in our day when our productivity is at its peak. A morning person hit more products, as it's said that sunrise is when you get active. Mostly from 8 o'clock to 10 o'clock. It's said that morning is the time when our minds work the sharpest. It provides you alertness and good memory ability. It is also called the "protected time." We get a new sense to think from, and then we get a sound vision of our steps and ideas to a routine of peak productivity.

Charles Duhigg is a known news reporter, works for the New York Times. He tells us to stop procrastinating and visualizing our next step in life. Not only does it give you confidence, but it also gives you a satisfactory feeling. You get an idea of the result, and you tend to do things more that way. This way, you get habitual of thinking about your next step beforehand. Habits are gradually formed. They are difficult to change but easy to assemble. A single practice can bring various elements from it. Those elements can help you learn the routine of an expert.

You will eventually fall into place. No one can change themselves in one day. Hard work is the key to any outcome. Productivity is the result of many factors but, an excellent daily routine is an integral part of it which we all need to follow. Once you fall into working constantly, you won't notice how productive you have become. It becomes a habit. There might be tough decisions along the way, which is typical for an average life. We need to focus on what's in front of us and start with giving attention to one single task on top of your priority list. That way, you can achieve more in less time. These are some factors and advice to start a daily routine for reaching the peak of productivity with the help of some great products.

Chapter 9:

<u>Gravitational Leadership</u>

Leadership.

It's not about position it is about disposition. It is not a title it is a role. A role you can take on from any place. Even if you are at the lowest point in the hierarchy – you can still lead. Leadership is not about being on the top rung, it is about holding ladders for others. It is not about having the most authority either. When a battalion went on a mission authorised by the King, the battalion did not have the King's authority, only his approval. Yet within them someone could still rise and lead the others. The beginning of your leadership is making decisions and taking action that gets approved by the people in authority. In doing that you will get noticed and over time trusted as an advisor. Sometimes the way you think and conduct yourself will enable you to lead people above you before you get any opportunity to lead people below you.

Because leadership is gravity.

Gravity does not push us downwards. It is not a force that comes from above us and holds us back.

Firstly, gravity does not push it pulls. Pulling involves leading by example and drawing people to you by virtue of your character. The good decisions that you make, the beneficial actions that you take, start to bundle together as a mass of admirable quality under your name. And gravity is just a reflection of mass. The more you engage and go all-in the faster that mass will grow – and with it your gravity will.

But gravity is not just something that attracts the people below you. Gravity doesn't pull downwards on a 2D plane, it pulls towards a centre. The people who are on the same level as you should be led by you as well. Not only that but you should be influencing the people above you. Not in such a way that you suck up to them but in a way that you stand out. Not necessarily even with the intention of climbing the ladder. Leadership must always be about leading in the space that you are without leaning towards the space you want to be. Allow promotions or advancements to flow naturally – if you try to force them then you will be detracting from your gravity and ultimately end up worse off.

Lastly, gravity does not hold people back, it keeps them grounded. Gravity is the force that enables us to walk forward, to move while retaining control. People who have been to space can testify to the lack of control experienced without gravity and the dangers therein. The markings of a leader is someone who is able to keep people grounded to the mission while still giving them freedom of movement. Gravity does not inhibit progress it gives it a better framework to work within. It allows people to pursue things with passion while staying within the borders of a greater purpose.

Such is the makings of a leader.

Chapter 10:
Fight Lethargy and Win

Life is a continuous grind. Life is the summation of our efforts. Life is a series of things that no one thinks can happen. But they do, and they do for a reason. Your life is no different than anyone else. You have the same needs and somewhat the same goals. But you might still be a failure while the world moves on. Let me explain why.

People always misunderstand having a humble mindset as opposed to having a go-getter mindset. The difference between you and a successful person is the difference in mindset.

When you think that you are not feeling well today to go to the gym. That you are not motivated enough to do some cardio or run that treadmill. That you didn't have a good day and now you are feeling down so you should stay in bed because you think you deserve some time off. This is the moment you messed up your life.

What you should have done is to tell yourself, What have I achieved today that made me deserving of this time off. You didn't!

How can you sit back and remain depressed when no one else feels sorry for you but only you do. Because you still haven't come to realize that no one will give you sympathy for something you made a mess of. And you are still not willing enough to make things happen for yourself.

When you have nothing, you think someone owes you something. That someone handles something bad that happens in your life. The reality is far from this.

It is fine if you are going through some rough patch in your life right now. But don't try to put the blame on others and back off of your responsibilities and duties. You have something to move towards but you are still sitting there waiting for the moment to come to your doorstep. But it ain't gonna happen. It's never an option to wait!

Don't just sit there and make strategies and set goals. Get up and start acting on those plans. The next plan will come by default.

You shouldn't feel depressed about the bad things, you should feel anger for why did you let those things happen to you in the first place. What did you lag that made you come to this stage right now. Why were you so lazy enough to let those results slide by you when your gut told you to do something different. But you didn't. And now it has all come to haunt you once again.

But you don't need that attitude. What you need is to stop analyzing and start doing something different rather than contemplate what you could have done.

The moments you lost will never come back, so there is no point in feeling sorry for those moments in this present moment. Use this moment to get the momentum you need.

Now is the time to prove yourself wrong, to make this life worth living for.

Now is the time to spend the most valuable asset of your life on something you want the most in your life. Now is the time to use all that energy and bring a change to your life that you will cherish for the rest of your life and in that afterlife.

Prove to yourself that you are worthy of that better life. That no one else deserves more than you. Because you made a cause for yourself. You ran all your life and struggled for that greater good.

Destiny carves its path when your show destiny what you have to offer.

You want to succeed in life, let me tell you the simplest way to that success; get up, go outside and get to work.

When you feel the lowest in your life, remember, you only start to lose that fat, when you start to sweat and you feel the heat and the pain coming through.

What you started yesterday, finish it today. Not tomorrow, not tonight, but right now!

Get working! It doesn't matter if it takes you an hour or 12 to complete the job. Do it. You will never fulfill the task if you keep thinking for the right moment. Every moment is the right moment.

You are always one decision away from a completely different life. You are always one moment away from the best moment of your life. But it is either this moment or it's never.

Chapter 11:
How Distraction Robs You of Joy

How many of you crave the satisfaction that distraction brings you? Whether it be checking your phone regularly for messages, or scrolling through social media apps such as Facebook, instagram, or even mindlessly browsing through streaming apps such as youtube or netflix in search of some form of content that can take your attention away from the work that is actually in front of you that you should be working on?

I believe that many of us crave these distractions because of a few key reasons. Let us see if any of these sound familiar to you, and after I've identified them i will tell you why distraction is actually not the answer to your problems.

The first reason is that we are probably bored and we want to fill that boredom with stuff just so that we can keep ourselves busy and to pass time. I would raise my hand and say that I am guilty of that.

The second reason is that we are probably subconsciously unhappy with what we are doing, whether it be our jobs, or our careers, we feel that we are not doing what we are meant to do and it is causing us anxiety, fear, and worry, and we turn to distractions as a form of therapy to try and calm our nerves, or just temporarily forget our problems for just enough time to feel good before we begin our work again. Does that sound like you?

The third reason is that we are just so engrossed in the new world of information consumption that we have become so addicted to our smartphones or smart appliances, that we willingly give 1/3 of our day away to be mindlessly consuming content that is not beneficial to our lives on this earth. The abundance of apps, streaming platforms, and mobile games, have given us a portal into another dimension away from the physical world. This distracts us from the important stuff we need to do every day to better our lives such as building meaningful relationships with friends, spending time with loved ones, and being present in whatever you are doing.

So why is distraction so harmful that it robs us of real joy and happiness?

From a physiological standpoint, distraction actually uses up a lot of our cognitive capacity to switch from a tasks which requires deep focus. When you are very productive, your brain is actually in a flow state of mind where productivity becomes much easier to achieve. You have undivided attention to complete the task at hand and your brain is working to the best of its ability to provide you with the information that you need to solve whatever problems the job requires. But when you receive a text or decide to take a quick break to check your phone and to scroll through social media, you are actually snapped out of that flow state of mind. And your mind goes into a passive state. And as you revert back to the task you were originally doing, not even mentioning the inertia and the amount of energy it takes to restart your work, your brain actually has to go through the painful process of connecting those cells from your working memory once again. costing you immense amounts of resources and energy. And as you do this probably tens of times each hour, you lose more and more of that focus and eventually you feel tired and unproductive.

And as you spiral downwards, your level of satisfaction drops and so does your sense of joy because you feel unaccomplished, you've wasted hours of time, and you may even start beating yourself up for such a poor performance.

So what action steps can you do to free yourself from distraction so that you can regain control of your energy and time?

Well the very first step, which is probably the simplest but harder to do, is to put your phone on silent mode, or keep it somewhere out of sight so that you are not tempted to reach for it. Turn off all possible forms of distraction that can jeopardise your workflow. And refrain from taking breaks as much as you can, even going to the toilet. Every minute you step away from what you are doing will cost you some form of energy in one way or another. You can even download the app "forest" which actually locks your phone down for a duration you have set for yourself, while at the same time planting a beautiful tree in your garden. It is quite rewarding to see that you have grown a tree after spending a full hour working. And as you feel more productive, your level of happiness will increase from the sense of accomplishment you feel that you got your work done in record time.

The next thing you can do is to start re-assessing the work you are doing. Ask yourself if you are truly happy at your job, because maybe u use distraction as an escape which could indicate that you are probably not doing what you were meant to do. If you really loved your job, you will be in a state of mind where your job doesn't even feel like job anymore and you just want to keep working because you are passionate about it. If that means changing your careers or trying something new, don't be afraid to do so.

The final step is to constantly remind yourself of the value of time and that time is not infinite. We only have so many hours in a day, do we really want to spend half of it on things on mindless content that does not improve ourselves as a person? Time is precious and we should spend it as wisely as we can, free of distraction, and doing meaningful work to better someone else's lives. And as we do these things, we can slowly start to regain control, which helps us become more self-disciplined. And this loop reinforces the good principles we should follow to achieve success and happiness.

Chapter 12:

Playing To Your Strengths

Have you ever asked yourself why you fail at everything you touch?
Why you seem to lack behind everyone you strive to beat?
Why you can't give up the things that are keeping you from achieving the goals you dream?
Has anyone told you the reason for all this?

You might wonder about it all your life and might never get to the right answer. Even though you stare at the answer every day in the mirror.

Yes! It's you! You are the reason for your failures.
You are the reason for everything bad going on in your life right now.
But you are also the master of your life, and you should start acting like one.

When the world brings you down, find another way to overcome the pressures.
Find another way to beat the odds.
Adverse situations only serve to challenge you.
Be mentally strong and bring the world to your own game.

Show the world what you are.
Show the world what you are capable of.

Don't let anyone dictate to you what you should do.
Rather shape your life to dictate the outcome with your efforts and skills.

You can't always be wrong.
Somewhere, and somehow, you will get the right answer.
That will be your moment to build what you lost.
That will be your moment to shut everyone else and rise high in the silence of your opponents.

If you don't get that chance, don't wait for it to come.
Keep going your way and keep doing the things you do best.
Paths will open to your efforts one day.

You can't be bad at everything you do.
You must be good at something.
Find out what works for you.
Find out what drives your spirit.
Find out what you can do naturally while being blind-folded with your hands tied behind your back.

There is something out there that is calling out to you.
Once you find it, be the best at it as you can.
It doesn't matter if you do not get to the top.
You don't anything to prove to anyone.
You only need one glimpse of positivity to show yourself that you have something worthwhile to live for.

Always challenge yourself.
If you did 5 hours of work today, do 7 tomorrow.
If you run 1 mile today, hit 3 by the end of the week.
You know exactly what you are capable of.
Play to your strengths.
Make it your motto to keep going every single day.

Make a decision.
Be decisive.
Stick with it.
Don't be afraid because there is nothing to fear.
The only thing to fear is the fear itself.

Tell your heart and your mind today, that you can't stop, and you won't stop.
Till the time you have the last breath in your lungs and the last beat in your heart, keep going.
You will need to put your heart out to every chance you can get to raise yourself from all this world and be invincible.

You have no other option but to keep going.
To keep trying until you have broken all the barriers to freedom.
You are unique and you know it.
You just need to have the guts to admit that you are special and live up to the person you were always meant to be.

Take stock of yourself today.

Where are you right now and where do you want to be?

The moment you realize your true goal, that is the moment you have unlocked your strengths.

Live your life on your terms.

Every dream that you dream is obtainable.

And the only way is to believe in yourself.

To believe that you are the only thing standing in the way of your past and your future.

Once you have started, tell yourself that there is no return.

Dictate your body to give up only when you have crossed the finish line.

Start acting on every whim that might get you to the ultimate fate.

These whims are your strength because you have them for a purpose.

Why walk when you can run?

Why run when you can fly?

Why listen when you can sing?

Why go out and dine when you can cook?

The biggest gift that you can give to yourself is the mental satisfaction that you provide yourself.

You are only limited to the extent you cage yourself.

The time you let go will be your salvation. But you have to let go!

Chapter 13:
<u>The Power of Developing Eye Contact with Your Client</u>

We've all heard the age-old saying the "eyes are the window to the soul," and in many ways, it holds. Everybody knows looking others in the eyes is beneficial in communication, but how important is eye contact, and how is it defined?

Eye contact can be subtle or even obvious. It can be a glaring scowl when a person is upset or a long glance when we see something off about someone else's appearance. It can even be a direct look when we are trying to express a crucial idea.

1) Respect

In Western countries like the United States, eye contact is critical <u>to show and earn respect</u>. From talking to your boss on the job or thanking your mom for dinner, eye contact shows the other person that you feel equal in importance.

There are other ways to show respect, but our eyes reflect our sincerity, warmth, and honesty.

This is why giving and receiving eye contact while talking is a surefire sign of a good conversation. Nowadays, it's common for people to glance at their phones no matter if they're in the middle of a conversation or not. That's why eye contact will set you apart and truly show that you give them your full and undivided attention.

2) Understanding

Sometimes locking glances is the only sign you need to show someone that you understand what they are talking about. More specifically, if you need to get a vital point across, eye contact is the best way to communicate that importance. Eye contact is also a form of background acknowledgment like saying "yeah" and "mhmm."
That means it shows the speaker that you are tuned in to and understand what they are saying.

3) Bonding

When someone is feeling an emotion or just performing a task, the same neurons that shine in their brain light up in someone else's brain who is watching them. This is because we have "mirror neurons" in our brains that are very sensitive to facial expressions and, most importantly, eye contact.

Direct eye contact is so powerful that it increases empathy and links together emotional states. Never underestimate the power of eye contact in creating long-lasting bonds.

4) Reveal Thoughts and Feelings

We have countless ways of describing eyes, including "shifty-eyed," "kind-eyed," "bright-eyed," "glazed over," and more. It's no wonder just about every classic love story starts with "two pairs of eyes meeting across the room." Eye contact is also a powerful form of simultaneous communication, meaning you don't have to take turns doing the communicating.

Ever wonder why poker players often wear sunglasses inside? It's because "the eyes don't lie." [We instinctually look into people's eyes](#) from birth to try and understand what they are thinking, and we continue to do it for life.

Chapter 14:
The Goal Is Not The Point

If you ever want to achieve your goals, stop thinking about them. I know this goes against everything anyone has ever said about achieving your goals.

Everyone says that think about one thing and then stick to it. Devote yourself to that one single goal as you are committed to your next breath. Check on your goals over and over again to see if you are still on track or not and you will get there sooner than you think.

What I am proposing is against all the theories that exist behind achieving your goals but wait a minute and listen to me.

The reason behind this opposing theory is that we spend more time concentrating on thinking and panning about our goals. Rather than actually doing something to achieve them.

We think about getting into college. Getting a Bachelor's degree and then getting our Master's degree and so on. So that we can finally decide to appear for an interview that we have dreamed about or to start a business that we are crazy about.

But these are not the requirements for any of them to happen. You can get a degree in whatever discipline you want or not, and can still opt for business. As far as job interviews are concerned, they are not looking for the most educated person for that post. But the most talented and experienced person that suits the role on hand.

So we purposefully spend our life doing things that carry the least importance in actual to that goal.

What we should be doing is to get started with the simplest things and pile upon them as soon as possible. Because life is too short to keep thinking.

Thinking is the easiest way out of our miseries. Staying idol and fantasizing about things coming to reality is the lamest thing to do when you can actually go out and start discovering the opportunities that lie ahead of you.

Your goals are things that are out of your control. You might get them, you might not. But the actions, motivation, and the effort you put behind your goal make the goal a small thing when you actually grab it. Because then you look back and you feel proud of yourself for what you have achieved throughout the journey.

At the end of that journey, you feel happier and content with what you gained within yourself irrespective of the goal. Because you made yourself realize your true potential and your true purpose as an active human being.

Find purpose in the journey for you can't know for sure about what lies ahead. But what you do know is that you can do what you want to do to your own limits. When you come to realize your true potential, the original goal seems to fade away in the background. Because then your effort starts to appear in the foreground.

A goal isn't always meant to be achieved as it might not be good for you in the end or in some other circumstances. But the efforts behind these goals serve as something to look back on and be amazed at.

Chapter 15:
Creating Successful Habits

Successful people have successful habits.
If you're stuck in life, feeling like you're not going anywhere, take a hard look at your habits.
Success is built from our small daily habits accumulated together,
Without these building blocks, you will not get far in life.
Precise time management, attention to detail, these are the traits of all who have made it big.
To change your life, you must literally change your life, the physical actions and the mindset.

Just as with success, the same goes with health.
Do you have the habit of a healthy diet and regular athletic exercises?
Healthy people have healthy habits.
If you are unhappy about your weight and figure, point the finger at your habits once again.

To become healthy, happy and wealthy, we must first become that person in the mind.
Success is all psychological.
Success has nothing to do with circumstances.
Until we have mastered the habits of our thinking we cannot project this success on the world.

We must first decide clearly who we want to be.
We must decide what our values are.
We must decide what we want to achieve.

Then we must discipline ourselves to take control of our destiny.

Once we know who we are and what we want to do,
Behaving as if it were reality becomes easy.

We must start acting the part.
That is the measure of true faith.
We must act as if we have already succeeded.
As the old saying goes: "fake it UNTIL YOU MAKE IT"

Commit yourself with unwavering faith.
Commit yourself with careful and calculated action.
You will learn the rest along the way

Every habit works towards your success or failure,
No matter how big or how small.
The more you change your approach as you fail, the better your odds become.
Your future life will be the result of your actions today.
It will be positive or negative depending on your actions now.

You will attain free-will over your thoughts and actions.
The more you take control, the happier you will be.

Guard your mind from negativity.
Your mind is your sanctuary.
Ignore the scaremongering.
Treat your mind to pure motivation.

We cannot avoid problems.
Problems are a part of life.
Take control of the situation when it arises.
Have a habit of responding with action rather than fear.

Make a habit of noticing everybody and respecting everybody.
Build positive relationships and discover new ideas.
Be strong and courageous, yet gentle and reasonable.
These are the habits of successful leaders.

Be meticulous.
Be precise.
Be focused.

Make your bed in the morning.
Follow the path of drill sergeants in the royal marines and US navy seals.
Simple yet effective,
This one habit will shift your mindset first thing as you greet the new day.

Choose to meditate.
Find a comfortable place to get in touch with your inner-self.
Make it a habit to give yourself clarity of the mind and spirit.
Visualize your goals and make them a reality in your mind.

Choose to work in a state of flow.
Be full immersed in your work rather than be distracted.
To be productive we need to have an incredible habit of staying focused.
It will pay off.
It will pay dividends.
The results will be phenomenal.

Every single thing you choose to make a habit will add up.
No matter how big or how small,
Choose wisely.

Choose the habit of treating others with respect.

Treat the cleaner the same as you would with investors and directors.
Treat the poor the same as you would with the CEO of a multi-national company.
Our habits and attitude towards ourselves and others makes up our character.

Choose a habit of co-operation over competition,
After all the only true competition is with ourselves.
It doesn't matter whether someone is doing better than us as long as we are getting better.
If someone is doing better we should learn from them.
Make it a habit of putting ourselves into someone else's shoes.
We might stand to learn a thing or two.

No habit is too big or too small.
To be happy and successful we must do our best in them all.

Chapter 16:
8 Ways On How To Start Taking Actions

Have you ever got caught up in situations when you can't bring yourself moving from deciding to doing? As a famous person once said, "Your beliefs become your thoughts; your thoughts become your words; your words become your actions; your actions become your habits; your habits become your values; your values become your destiny."

The first step towards success is by taking action. If you keep on thinking that you have to lose weight, start a business, learn a new language, or get another degree, you will end up nowhere without executing these thoughts into actions.

Here are 8 Ways To Start Moving The Needle In Your Life:

1. Decide that you want to get out of your comfort zone

The fear that we have that doesn't allow us to take action is that we might have to sacrifice our comfort zone in the process. And trust me, a lot of people aren't willing to do that. But if you don't step out of your comfort zone, how will you determine your true potential? You don't need the motivation to start taking action, and you just have to gather your willpower, stop with the excuses and procrastination, and get moving!

2. Don't indulge in the habit of Hesitatation

Have you had a great idea but then decide 10 minutes later that it was stupid. Ever wondered why that was? The answer is quite simple and straightforward; hesitation. We dwell on hesitation for too long. This makes it very difficult for us to get started on something. Thinking will only lead us to more and more thinking, which will lead us to a loop of continual thoughts, and our actions will get dominated by them. And then the regret that follows us is usually, "Why didn't we start earlier?" David Joseph Schwartz once said, "To fight fear, act. To increase fear – wait, put off, postpone."

3. Stop waiting for the perfect time:

There's a Chinese proverb that says, "The best time to plant a tree was 20 years ago. The second-best time is now." It means that there is no such thing as perfect timing. The minute we start to take action, the time becomes perfect. If we wait till everything gets in order or becomes exemplary, then we will be waiting forever. The ideal time in your eyes was last year, but the second-best time is right here and right now. It's never too late to start with your goals, dreams, and passions. All we have in our hands is the present time and what counts is how efficiently we spend this time. We must take action now and make adjustments along the way if we feel like it.

4. Don't pause and wait:

Have you ever found yourself thinking that, hey, it's a good day to wander around the city, but found yourself sitting and wasting time watching TV? Or you thought of doing your assignment but got caught up in a more hopeless task? Or you thought of presenting a new idea to your boss but got shied away? All of these thoughts, no matter how positive they were, stand nowhere unless you implement them. So stop being a talker and start being a doer. A doer is someone who immediately moves forward with his ideas. When we pause and look around, we will find ourselves making excuses and allow doubts to creep through into our minds. "The most difficult thing is the decision to act; the rest is merely tenacity." - Amelia Earhart.

5. Stop Over-thinking:

There's always an endless loop of overthinking that we can't get over with no matter how hard we try. From imagining the worst-case scenarios of even the best situations to getting anxious and depressed whenever any minor inconvenience happens, our mind tricks us into thinking that we can never get the best of both worlds (HM fans, I gotcha!) When we overthink stuff, we tend to get paralysis of analysis. We start to analyze every situation and obsess over how things aren't perfect, or the conditions aren't going our way. We question the amount of time that we have to commit and make endless excuses and reasons not to move forward with whatever we want to do.

6. Take continuous action:

The first step is the hardest step that we have to take. But once you get started, make sure that you fully commit yourself to your goal. Take continuous actions and keep up with your momentum by doing something related to your plan every day. Even if you are scheduling only 15-20 minutes of your life completing a small task, it will eventually add up into the more remarkable things. Moreover, it will help you build confidence by seeing your achievements. "It does not matter how slowly you go as long as you do not stop." - Confucius.

7. Overcome your fears:

We often succumb to our fears before even taking a step. The fear of failure, of not being good enough, of not doing enough, is the most common among them. Our mind tricks us into thinking that we might end up failing sooner or later. This prevents us from taking the first step and implementing our thoughts into actions. For example, suppose you're a professional speaker at a public speaking event. You have gained loads of experience, and you have no problem speaking to the lobby. But you do feel yourself getting nervous when you have to wait around for your turn. However, once you get started, all that fear and anxiety disappear. If you face similar situations in life, start being a doer, take action towards it and see how it will boost your confidence.

8. Eliminate any distractions:

We live in a world where distractions and procrastination have become more important than productivity. Have you ever found yourself thinking that you will take the online lecture for the subject you have been struggling with but ended up checking your social media accounts or watching irrelevant videos on YouTube? Procrastination is the primary reason we never end up doing what we should keep in our priorities. Instead, we should focus on our tasks, eliminate all the distractions and start with a slow but steady pace towards our goal. A single average idea put into action is far more valuable than those 20 genius ideas saved for another day or another time.

Conclusion:

Achieving your goals and dreams isn't an overnight task but takes years and decades to give you the final fruits. It's a road that will have setbacks, obstacles, lessons, and challenges. But what matters is that we shouldn't give up. We should face all the struggles and not surrender ourselves to our fears and demotivation. Converting your thoughts into actions and then enjoying the journey will equip you to thrive and see your goals become a reality in no time. So take into account what steps you took today. No matter how small they may be, appreciate and celebrate them.

Chapter 17:
<u>Why You've Come Too Far To Quit</u>

Remember the first day of school, when someone bullied you for being too nerdy, or for being too whiny. What did you feel when some called you a Four-eye for wearing glasses? What did you do then? How did you answer them? You didn't! Right? Why?

Because you weren't strong enough then to tackle anyone. Because you didn't have any experience to tell you what to do next.

But your parents told you to stop crying and keep doing your thing and one day, everything will be secondary. So you kept your line, didn't indulge in anything anyone else said and you got through that time.

This is the definition of life. Life is a sequence of events that bully you at every corner. But you cannot give up on life, because someone put a dent on your new car or if someone spilled coffee on your shirt.

Things happen because life happens, and you live your life for the things you want to achieve one day.

You dream because you hope for a better future, and that future is worth living for if you have suffered and felt the pain.

Nothing in this life is easy, but nothing is impossible. It may not be possible for you but at the same moment it might be happening for someone else in the world

You have come this far, to achieve the goals your set. You can't give up now only because you haven't seen it yet.

You breathe every day because you have to. Your success has the same needs! You need to give life everything that you got. Not on some days, but every day because it is not something you do when you feel like it, but you have to because you have to live on your terms. No one can dictate your life but only you.

When you feel like quitting, remember why you started it all. You started it to prove everyone wrong. You started it to shun your haters. You started to bully the bullies.

When you feel like quitting, remember, you have too much to fight for and very little to quit for.

When you get up in the morning, remember what you dreamt of last night. Remember your failures and give yourself a chance to prove yourself wrong.

Quitting is for those who are still the kid they were back then. Quitting is for those who still have the feeling that everything will get better on its own - It never does, and it never will. Only if you quit the quitting attitude and start taking initiative for your ultimate dream.

The best you can be is by the best effort you put into being the protagonist of your story. Become the writer of your story. If you want your story to remain average, remain the same person you were a day before.

If your heart tells you to quit, rev up your heart to do one pick one more step towards your penultimate goal. Dictate your heart how bad do you want it.

If you are still the kid who still thinks that things will happen no matter what I do, believe me, you are wrong. This whole attitude of not trying hard enough to achieve your goals is the biggest thing wrong with an average human. But you are not an average human.

The average human wouldn't have the guts to pursue the dream in the first place. An average human wouldn't dream big in the first place. An average human would have given up on the first setback of life and went down a deep hole, only to avoid the problems. But it never is the solution to anything.

Build the guts to keep going no matter what happens. Life will beat you up at every interval. You might have a big setback after every brief moment of happiness.

You might lose friends, family, and everyone you ever cared for. People who were once standing shoulder to shoulder with you might not even care to say your name if they think you don't need what you are striving for. But they don't have a say in your future. It's you who has everything to care for. Everything to account for. So don't give up only because everyone else gave up on you. You are still alive and trying.

Give yourself every chance, to win. Give your life every chance for it to matter. Avail every stone to keep the bullies away, but not by mirroring the act, but your efforts for your goal and they will bow down one day.

Chapter 18:
Becoming High Achievers

By becoming high achievers we become high off life, what better feeling is there than aiming for something you thought was unrealistic and then actually hitting that goal.
What better feeling is there than declaring we will do something against the perceived odds and then actually doing it.
To be a high achiever you must be a believer,
You must believe in yourself and believe that dream is possible for you.
It doesn't matter what anyone else thinks , as long as you believe,
To be a high achiever we must hunger to achieve.
To be an action taker.
Moving forward no matter what.
High achievers do not quit.
Keeping that vision in their minds eye until it becomes reality, no matter what.
Your biggest dream is protected by fear , loss and pain.
We must conquer all 3 of these impostors to walk through the door.
Not many do , most are still fighting fear and if they lose the battle, they quit.

Loss and pain are part of life.
Losses are hard on all of us.
Whether we lose possessions, whether we lose friends, whether we lose our jobs, or whether we lose family members.
Losing doesn't mean you have lost.
Losses are may be a tough pill to swallow, but they are essential because we cannot truly succeed until we fail.
We can't have the perfect relationship if we stay in a toxic one, and we can't have the life we desire until we make room by letting go of the old.

The 3 imposters that cause us so much terror are actually the first signs of our success. So walk through fear in courage , look at loss as an eventual gain, and know that the pain is part of the game and without it you would be weak.

Becoming a high achiever requires a single minded focus on your goal, full commitment and an unnatural amount of persistence and work.

We must define what high achievement means to us individually, set the bar high and accept nothing less.

The achievement should not be money as money is not our currency but a tool.

The real currency is time and your result is the time you get to experience the world's places and products , so the result should always be that.

The holiday home , the fast car and the lifestyle of being healthy and wealthy, those are merely motivations to work towards. Like Carrots on a stick.

High achievement is individual to all of us, it means different things to each of us,

But if we are going to go for it we might as well go all out for the life we want, should we not?

I don't think we beat the odds of 1 in 400 trillion to be born, just to settle for mediocrity, did we?

Being a high achiever is in your DNA , if you can beat the odds , you can beat anything.

It is all about self-belief and confidence, we must have the confidence to take the action required and often the risk.

Risk is difficult for people and it's a difficult tight rope to walk. The line between risk and recklessness is razor thin.

Taking risks feels unnatural, not surprisingly as we all grew up in a health and safety bubble with all advice pointing towards safe and secure ways.

But the reward is often in the risk and sometimes a leap of blind faith is required. This is what stops most of us - the fear of the unknown.

The truth is the path to success is foggy and we can only ever see one step ahead , we have to imagine the result and know it's somewhere down this foggy path and keep moving forward with our new life in mind.

Know that we can make it but be aware that along the path we will be met by fear , loss and pain and the bigger our goal the bigger these monsters will be.

The top achievers financially are fanatical about their work and often work 100+ hours per week.

Some often work day and night until a project is successful.

Being a high achiever requires giving more than what is expected, standing out for the high standard of your work because being known as number 1 in your field will pay you abundantly.

Being an innovator, thinking outside the box for better practices, creating superior products to your competition because quality is more rewarding than quantity.

Maximizing the quality of your products and services to give assurance to your customers that your company is the number 1 choice.

What can we do differently to bring a better result to the table and a better experience for our customers?

We must think about questions like that because change is inevitable and without thinking like that we get left behind, but if we keep asking that, we can successfully ride the wave of change straight to the beach of our desired results.

The route to your success is by making people happy because none of us can do anything alone, we must earn the money and to earn it we must make either our employers or employees and customers happy.

To engage in self-promotion and positive interaction with those around us, we must be polite and positive with everyone, even with our competition.

Because really the only competition is ourselves and that is all we should focus on.

Self-mastery, how can I do better than yesterday?

What can I do different today that will improve my circumstances for tomorrow.

Little changes add up to a big one.

The belief and persistence towards your desired results should be 100%, I will carry on until… is the right attitude.

We must declare to ourselves that we will do this , we don't yet know how but we know that we will.

Because high achievers like yourselves know that to make it you must endure and persist untill you win.

High achievers have an unnatural grit and thick skin , often doing what others won't, putting in the extra hours when others don't.

After you endure loss and conquer pain , the sky is the limit, and high achievers never settle until they are finished.

Chapter 19:

5 Ways To Deal with Personal Feelings of Inferiority

Have you at some point felt that you are inferior to others? That's normal. All of us, at some point in our lives, have felt the same. Growing up, we saw other kids who performed better than us in the class. Kids who played sports well. Kids who were loved by all. We got jealous. We felt inferior to them. We constantly compared ourselves to them.

Almost everyone has experienced that in their childhood. But do you still feel the same about others? Do you constantly analyze situations and people around you? Do you feel worthless? Then you probably have an inferiority complex. But the good news is you can get over this inferiority complex. We are going to list some of the things that will help you in doing that.

1. **Build self-confidence**

Treat yourself better. Act confident. Do what you love. Embrace yourself. Is there anything in your body that you don't feel confident about? Maybe your smile, your nose, or your hair? The trick here is to either accept yourself the way you are or do something about it. If you have curly hair, get your hair straightener. Do whatever makes you feel better about yourself.

2. Surround yourself with people who uplift you

It's important to realize that your inferiority complex might be linked to the people around you. It might be your relatives, your friends at college, your siblings, or your colleagues. Analyze your interactions with them.

Once you can identify people who try to pull you down, do not reciprocate your feelings, or are not very encouraging, start distancing yourself from them. Look for positive people, who uplift you, and who bring out the better version of yourself. Take efforts to develop a relationship with them.

3. Stop worrying about what other people think.

One major cause of inferiority complexes is constantly thinking about what others are thinking about us. We seek validation from them for every action of ours. Sometimes we are thinking about their actions, while sometimes, we imagine what they think.

4. Stop worrying about what other people think.

One major cause of inferiority complexes is constantly thinking about what others are thinking about us. We seek validation from them for every action of ours. Sometimes we are thinking about their actions, while sometimes, we are imagining what they think.

Disassociate yourself from their judgments. It's ultimately your opinion about yourself that matters. When we feel good about ourselves, others feel good about ourselves.

5. **Do not be harsh on yourself.**

There is no need to be harsh on yourself. Practice self-care. Love yourself. Be kind to yourself. Do not over-analyze situations. Do not expect yourself to change overnight. Give yourself time to heal.

Chapter 20:
Being Open To Opportunities For Social Events

As we continue from the previous video, something I learned is that things never turn out as how you would expect to in life. And the more we try to force something, the more resistance we face. And the more we take things in stride and just trust the process, the more things tend to flow naturally. You will see what I mean as we go through this video together.

As I was describing about how my social life was basically non existent at one point, if you guys haven't watched that video, do check it out first.

After taking a hard look at the decisions I made that left me with little to no social support or events to go to, i knew that I needed to do a 180 if i hoped to see any sort of rebound in my social life. And I started making a concrete plan with specific actions that would put me in a favourable position to attract and keep new friends.

At my lowest point, I knew that there was little that I could do to salvage my previous relationships, that I had probably done irreparable harm to them and i needed to start all over again. And that is to Make new friends from scratch. It wasn't so much something that I felt i needed right away, but i knew that in the long run, investing in friendships would bring me much more joy than money ever could especially in the latter years of my life. I knew that money wasn't the end all be all, and that people was the way to go.

Money can be made, but friendships cannot be bought.

I started the goal of dedicating this year and beyond to new friendships and began by signing up for activities that were in line with my interests. As an avid tennis fan and a player of the game, i decided that that was where i would begin. I started joining tennis groups and started playing games with complete strangers. Having also a growing interest in yoga and working out, I also started going for classes with my membership. Whilst i did not really make any real friends right away, I felt that I was already connected in some ways to people with similar interests. And I felt like i was part of a community, that I belonged somewhere. The more i showed up for these activities, the more people kept seeing me around, and the more these people started associated me as being regulars. Soon I was invited by one or two people to join a private game and that in itself became a regular thing. I started seeing these faces weekly for a year and we became friends naturally over the game of tennis. Yoga was a different story as it was more of an individual kind of sport, and people were generally more focused on their own practice on the mat, but it was fine as my interest for yoga faded pretty quickly anyway.

At the gym I started making one or two friends as well. It became natural to chat up with the gym regulars and even the staff, i felt like i looked forward to attending these events not because I wanted to work out, but because I enjoyed the social part and meeting my new friends and striking up random conversations.

For those of you who work in 9-5 jobs, you might not face this same issue as me, as meeting new people and colleagues would be a very simple way to start making new aquaintances that could potentially turn into friends... Seeing that you would meet them every single day whether you liked it or not. But for people who work from home or who are self employed, we do need to make the extra effort to meet new people.

As my pool of friends grew bigger, I started forming my own private tennis group, putting in the extra effort to book the courts day in and out, and inviting them to play. Eventually all my hard work paid off, as people reciprocated by inviting me to their own private outings and dinners. And I started to integrate into their lives and their friends. I had made myself so readily available, not by design, but by choice because at that point I was so ready to say yes to anything it became so natural to prioritise hanging out over just simply working all day and night. My friends saw me as someone they could count on to be there and they had no qualms making me a priority when they wanted to find somebody to hang out with. I reciprocated by making them a priority as well. And the friendship blossomed from there.

For the first time in a long time, I felt truly alive. I felt that my life had a purpose, it had balance, it had work and play, there was yin to my yang, and i looked forward to working as much as I looked forward to hanging out.

I don't know how long this bliss will last, but i know that I had made the right choice. This all happened in 2020, smack in the middle of the pandemic, and yet I made it work because I had given myself every opportunity to succeed.

If this story resonated with you, then i challenge each and everyone of you today to simply decide on a time and place you would like to begin changing the areas of your life that you find lacking. The one thing that I have learned from all this is that it is never tooo late to turn things around. Whether it be financial, emotional, or physical. A firm decision to change is all it takes. And giving it time to grow and blossom is essential to seeing long term success.

I hope you have learned something today and I wish you all the best in putting yourself in positions where opportunities would arise. Take care and I'll see you in the next one.

Chapter 21:
Develop A Habit of Studying

Life is a series of lessons.
Your education does not end at 16 or 18 or 21,
It has only just begun.
You are a student of life.
You are constantly learning, whether you know it or not.

You have a free will of what you learn and which direction you go.
If you develop a habit of studying areas of personal interest,
your life will head in the direction of your interests.
If you study nothing you will be forced to learn and change through tragedy and negative circumstances.

What you concentrate on you become,
so study and concentrate on something that you want.
If you study a subject for just one hour per day, in a year you would of studied 365 hours, making you a national expert.
If you keep it up for 5 years, that's 1825 hours , making you an international expert, all from one hour per day.

If you commit to two hours you will half that time.
Studying is the yellow brick road to your dream life.

Through concentration and learning you will create that life.
Knowledge opens doors.
Being recognised as an expert increases pay.
Not studying keeps you were you are –
Closed doors and a stagnant income.

If you don't learn anything how can you expect to be valuable?
If you don't grow how can you expect to be paid more?
It only becomes too late to learn when you are dead;
until then the world is an open book will billions of pages.

Often what we deem impossible is in fact possible.
Often even your most lofty dreams you haven't even scratched the surface of what you are capable of.

Taylor your study to your goal –
follow the yellow brick road of your design.
Follow the road you have built and walk toward your goals.

If you want to be successful, study success and successful people,
then learn everything you can about your chosen field.
Plan your day with a set time for your study.
I don't care how busy you claim to be,
everybody can spare 1 hour out of 24 to work on themselves.
If not , I hope you're happy where you are,
because that is about as far as you will get without learning more.

Studying is crucial to success whether it's formal
or learning from books and online material at home.
The knowledge you learn will progress you towards your dream life.
If that is not worth an hour or two per day,
then maybe you don't want it enough and that's ok.
Maybe you want something different to what you thought,
or maybe you're happy where you are.

If not, it's on you to do this –
for yourself,
for your family,
and for your partner in life.
It's up to you to create the world you want –
A world that only you know if you deserve.

You must learn the knowledge and build the dream
because the world needs your creation.
Be a keen student of life and apply its lesson
to build your future on a solid and safe foundation.

Chapter 22:
8 Common Mistakes That Cause You to Make Bad Decisions

Are you too much of a perfectionist? Do you overestimate your abilities? Do you trust intuition too much? Are you overpowered by past decisions, even if they've been proven to be flawed? Let's hone in on ten mistakes we all make so that we may learn to stop tripping over the same stones repeatedly.

1. **Holding Out For The Perfect Decision**

Striving for perfection in our decisions adds unnecessary pressure and often leads to "analysis paralysis." No one likes to be wrong, but we must shake our fear and accept that decision-making means taking risks: sometimes we'll get it right, other times we won't. Mistakes are a part of learning.

"I've failed over and over and over again in my life. And that is why I succeed," boasts Michael Jordan, arguably the best basketball player of all time.

2. Failing To Face Reality

We tend to see things as we would like them to be, confusing wishful thinking with reality. For example, 75 percent of drivers think they are above average behind the wheel, which is statistically impossible.

Faced with a situation, we tend to take a stance and may fail to see beyond it, ignoring what might be better options out there. Furthermore, we tend to magnify the positive aspects of our stance and minimize the negative ones. One good way to avoid this bias is to try and distinguish facts (objective) from opinions (subjective).

3. Falling For Self-Deceptions

The way we are presented with a situation, and the way we present it to ourselves, affects our final decisions. For example, when some cancer patients were told that the survival rate one year after surgery was 68 percent, a significant percentage opted for that surgery. Meanwhile, when others were told that 32 percent of patients die within a year of the operation, no one elected to undergo it. The same information was given, just presented differently.

To avoid falling prey to self-deception, it is important to seek alternatives and consider them from different angles. Finally, sleep on it before making the decision.

4. Going With The Flow

There is something worse than being wrong: being the only one who is wrong. Doing what everyone else does is easier and, more importantly, may save us from embarrassment. Hence our tendency to follow the herd, even if it is heading to a precipice.

We saw this with the dot-com bubble, for example. Everyone wanted to invest in tech companies when the bubble inflated, even when most investors knew little about them.

The problem with imitation (and not thinking before deciding) is that we eliminate the possibility of finding wiser alternatives than what is fashionable.

5. Rushing and Risking Too Much

Before deciding hastily, we should consider whether a decision is truly urgent. We tend to rush into things, crossing things off our list to feel accomplished. But all we're doing in a rush is taking unnecessary risks.

For example, the Chernobyl disaster was caused by an unnecessary test that simulated a power failure at the nuclear power plant. The outcome was exactly what they sought to avoid by going through the motions for security testing: the reactor exploded. There was no urgent need to run that test, but it happened anyway, risking far too much.

6. Relying Too Heavily on Intuition

Intuition can be an asset, but it leads to mistakes when we allow it to outweigh analytical thinking. What's more, testing our hunches with low-cost experiments is important.

The authors offer Samsung chairman Lee Kun-hee as a cautionary tale. In the 1990s, he reportedly decided to get into automobile manufacturing because he "sensed" the market would take off in Asia. The project resulted in a loss of $2 billion and 50,000 layoffs.

7. Being Married To Our Ideas

It's hard for us to change a prior decision, even if keeping the status quo is inefficient or harmful.

The year 2003 saw the grounding of the Concorde, a supersonic jet airliner that was never profitable. But it took a fatal accident, with over 100 fatalities, to put it into permanent retirement. Economically speaking, the right decision should have been made long before then, but that meant acknowledging a failure. And no one likes doing that.

8. Paying Little Heed to Consequences

Sometimes we don't consider the consequences of a decision. Or we only consider the most direct and immediate ones, ignoring the side effects. And that can cause even bigger problems than the ones we were trying to solve in the first place.

That's what happened to those in charge of the Titanic, who wanted to arrive at their destination 24 hours ahead of schedule to silence critics who claimed their large ship would be slow. They ignored warnings about icebergs, warnings that should have slowed them down for safety's sake.

Chapter 23:

Be Motivated by Challenge

You have an easy life and a continuous stream of income, you are lucky! You have everything you and your children need, you are lucky! You have your whole future planned ahead of you and nothing seems to go in the other direction yet, you are lucky!

But how far do you think this can go? What surety can you give yourself that all will go well from the start to the very end?

Life will always have a hurdle, a hardship, a challenge, right there when you feel most satisfied. What will you do then?

Will you give up and look for an escape? Will you seek guidance? Or will you just give up and go down a dark place because you never thought something like this could happen to you?

Life is full of endless possibilities and an endless parade of challenges that make life no walk in the park.

You are different from any other human being in at least one attribute. But your life isn't much different than most people's. You may be less fortunate or you may be the luckiest, but you must not back down when life strikes you.

This world is a cruel place and a harsh terrain. But that doesn't mean you should give up whenever you get hit in the back. That doesn't mean you don't catch what the world throws at you.

Do you know what you should do? Look around and observe for examples. Examples of people who have had the same experiences as you had and what good or bad things did they do? You will find people on both extremes.

You will find people who didn't have the courage or guts to stand up to the challenge and people who didn't have the time to give up but to keep pushing harder and harder, just to get better at what they failed the last time.

The challenges of life can never cross your limits because the limits of a human being are practically infinite. But what feels like a heavy load, is just a shadow of your inner fear dictating you to give up.

But you can't give up, right? Because you already have what you need to overcome this challenge too. You just haven't looked into your backpack of skills yet!

If you are struggling at college, go out there and prove everyone in their wrong. Try to get better grades by putting in more hours little by little.

If people take you as a non-social person, try to talk to at least one new person each day.

If you aren't getting good at a sport, get tutorials and try to replicate the professionals step by step and put in all your effort and time if you truly care for the challenge at hand.

The motivation you need is in the challenge itself. You just need to realize the true gains you want from each stone in your path and you will find treasures under every stone.

Chapter 24:
Don't Wait Another Second To Live Your Dreams

We often think we must be ready to act , but the truth is we will never be ready while we wait.

We only become ready by walking the path, and battles are seldom won in ideal circumstances.

Money is not the real currency in life , the real currency is time and every second we wait is a second we waste.

Your biggest motivator is the ticking clock and the impending reality that one day it will be too late.

Your biggest fear is getting to 80 and realising you haven't lived, that you haven't done what you wanted in life because of fear.

True regret is a medicine none of us want to taste.

We must decide what we really want, set the bar high , go after it now and accept nothing less.

You deserve respect, but you will live what you expect, this life will pay you any price but it's up to you what you accept.

You must act now from where we are with what we have , right now , not tomorrow or next week , right now.

Take the first step , make the draft plan .

Find out what knowledge you need to make this dream a reality.

Taking action now towards the goal in mind is crucial, if we wait we risk losing the drive to make things happen.

We can never be fully ready because we don't know what exactly is going to happen, a lot of it is learned along the way - especially if you're doing something brand new.

If not, reading what has been done before in your area will give you a good understanding of what might work.

Every second we spend thinking about, instead of acting towards our goal is wasted time.

You cannot afford to wait because if you do not act , someone else will , someone else could also be thinking what you're thinking and act first.

Those who wait for opportunity will wait in vain because opportunity must be created, first in the mind, then in the world.

We cannot see the vast opportunity that surrounds us unless we believe it is there, believe it is possible and act on that belief, at the time it arises.

The world is pliable and opportunities do not wait for people to be ready. You must become ready on the road.

The obstacles you have to overcome on the move will mould you into the person you need to be to reach your biggest goals.

You must be patient, to be practitioners of who you believe you will be one day.

Getting into the mindset of whoever you want to be right now, because until you become that person in mind, you cannot in body.

As we start acting differently, different actions bring different results and if the new actions are positive and aimed at a certain goal , just like magic the world begins to transform for you, towards the life you wanted.

The leap of faith is acting now, feeling unready aiming for something that may seem unrealistic, but this is an essential leap and test to be overcome. As the days go on with the goal in mind , it will seem to become more likely and you will feel more ready until it feels definite.

All things are possible but there will be required ingredients to your success you might not know yet, so the first step is to gain the knowledge required.

Once you begin to learn that knowledge you are on the road to your goal. Organization and optimization of your time will make it easier to be efficient.

If time is the real currency, are you getting good value for what you spend your time doing?

If not , is it not time you used some of your seconds working towards something phenomenal?

You only have so many and it is losing value every day as we age, think about it.

We must create a sense of urgency because it is urgent if you want to succeed in an ever changing world.

If we wait our ideas, products and services may become irrelevant because new technology and innovation is always changing.

Our ideas are only viable when they come ,

Strike while the iron is hot is good advice ,

When the ambition and goal is strongest and clearest.

Clarity is essential when pursuing dreams and goals, every detail of your dream should be clear in your mind down to the sights , colours and smells.

When we think about our goal we should feel it as if it's already here, and start acting like it is.

Dress talk and walk as if you are that person now.

Whatever our current circumstances everyone has the ability to build in their minds, set the goal then determine the first step.

If your circumstances are bad there are more steps, but there are steps.

Start from step one and walk in confidence always keeping the big dream in mind knowing that this can happen for you.

We have a waking mind and a subconscious mind.

The subconscious knows things we don't, it is responsible for our gut instinct, which always seems to be right so follow that .

Everyday listening to that voice , keeping a clear vision of your goal in your mind and confidently taking action towards it.

It's possible for you if you act ,

But time is ticking.

Chapter 25:
Do The Painful Things First

There are a lot of secret recipes to be happier; one of them is; seek what's painful first. Sure, this may sound a little ironic, but you will be surprised to know that all scientific research is behind this. Behavioral scientists discovered that one of the most effective ways to create an enjoyable experience is to stack the painful parts of the experience early in the process. For example, if you're a doctor, a lawyer, accountant, etc., it's better to break bad news first and then finish with the good news. This will give the clients a more satisfying experience since you start poorly then end on a solid note instead of starting well and ending badly.

There's a couple of crucial reasons why we should do the painful things first. We know that we have limited willpower during the day, and we also know that the most painful activities or tasks are sometimes the most difficult ones. So if we complete the things we find the most difficult first, we'll be exerting less energy on less complicated activities for the rest of the day. Scientific studies show that our prefrontal cortex (creative part of the brain) is the most active the moment we wake up. At the same time, the analytical parts of our brain (the editing and proofreading parts) become more active as the day goes on.

Another reason to do the painful activities firsthand after you wake up is that you would be freed from all the distractions and tend to do these tasks more quickly. If you delay the complex tasks, it will only come back to bite you. Starting with only one task for a day can be enough, as it could lead you to achieve more of them as time goes by. Things like building a new business, losing weight, or learning a new skill require pain and slow work in the beginning to get momentum. But after some persistence, you will likely see your improvements. Behavioral psychology suggests that we're more likely to lead a happier life if we're making improvements over time. Anthony Robbins once said, "If you're not growing, you're dying."

Making slow but gradual improvements is where persistency comes in. It's going to be painful and frustrating initially, and you won't learn a new language in an instant, or your business won't thrive immediately. But when you decide to sacrifice your short-term pleasure for a future pay-off, you will get to enjoy the long-term benefits over a sustained period. Stop avoiding what's hard; embrace it for your long-term happiness.

Chapter 26:
7 Ways To Know If You're A Good Person

This question is something that we wonder from time to time. When we are at our lowest point and we look around, there could be a chance that there may not be that many people in our lives that we can really count on.

We start to wonder how people actually see us. Are we good people? Have we been nice to those around us? Or do we come off as pretentious and hence people tend to stay clear of us for some reason.

There is a dilemma lately about the use of social media and having followers. It seems that people are interested in following your socials, but when it comes to you asking them out or chatting them up, they don't respond or are uninterested to meet up with you.

You then start to wonder if there is something wrong with you. You start to question your morals, your self-worth, and everything about your life. This can quickly spiral out of control and lead to feelings that you are somehow flawed.

Today we're going to help you answer that question: Am I a good person? Here are 7 Ways To Find Out If You Are Indeed One

1. Look At The People Who Have Stuck Around

I think this one is a good place to start for all of us. Instead of wondering if we have gone wrong somewhere, take a look at the friends and family who have stuck around for you over all this time. They are still there for you for a reason. You must have done something right for them not to leave you for other people. Sure some of them may not be as close as they once were, but they are still there. Think about the people who celebrate your birthdays with you, the people who still asks if you want to hang out from time to time, and the people who you can count on in times of emergency. We may not be able to determine if we are good people from this, but we know that at least we are not so far off the rails.

2. Ask Them To Be Honest With You

If you really want to find out if you are a good person, ask your friends directly and honestly, to point out to you areas that they feel you need to work on. Sometimes we cannot see the flaws and the misguided actions that we portray to the world. People may gradually dislike and drift away from us quietly without telling us why. The people who have stuck around know you best, so let them be brutally honest with you. Take what they have to say as constructive criticism, rather than a personal attack on your character. It is better to know in what areas you lack as a person and to work to improve it, than to go through life obliviously and thinking that there is absolutely nothing wrong with you.

3. Think About Why Your Friends May Not Respond To Your Messages

Many a times friendships simply run its natural course. As work, relationships, and family come into the picture, it is inevitable that people drift apart over time. If you decide to hit your friends up and they don't respond, don't take it too personally. It could be that maybe you're just not a vital piece of the puzzle in their lives anymore. If their friendships aren't one that you have been cultivating anyway, you may want to consider removing them completely from your lives. Find new people who will appreciate and love you rather than dwell on the past. There may be nothing wrong with you as a person, it's just the cruel nature of time playing its dirty game.

4. Keeping It Real With Yourself

Do you think that you are a good person? The fact that you are here shows that you may already have an inclination that something may not be quite right with you but you can't quite put a finger on it. Instead of looking for confirmation from external sources, try looking within. Ask yourself the hard questions. Think about every aspect of your life and evaluate yourself. If you have more enemies than friends, maybe there is something you aren't doing quite right that needs some work. Write those possible flaws down and see if you can work through them.

5. Do You Try Your Best To Help Others?

Sometimes we may not be great friends but we may be great at other things, such as being passionate about a cause or helping other people. Maybe friendships aren't a priority for us and hence it is not a good indicator of whether we are good people by looking at the quality of our friendships. If instead we are driven by a cause bigger than ourselves, and we participate through volunteering, events, and donation drives, we can pat ourselves on the back and say that at least we have done something meaningful to better the lives of others. In my opinion you are already a winner.

6. Is Life Always About What You Want?

This one could be a red flag because if we create a life that is only centred around us, we are in danger of being self-obsessive. Having the "Me First" attitude isn't something to be proud of. Life is about give and take, and decisions should be made fairly for all parties involved. If you only want to do things your way, or go to places you want, at the expense of the opinions of others, you are driving people away without realising it. Nobody likes someone who only thinks about themselves. If you catch yourself in this position, it may be time to consider a 180 turn.

7. People Enjoy Being Around You

While this may not be the best indicator that you are a good person, it is still a decent way to tell if you are well-liked and if people enjoy your presence. Generally people are attracted to others who are kind, loyal, trustworthy, and charismatic. If people choose to ask you out, they could find you to be one of those things, which is a good sign that you're not all too bad. Of course you could have ulterior motives for presenting yourself in a well-liked manner, but disingenuity usually gets found out eventually and you very well know if you are being deceitful to others for your own personal gain.

Conclusion

There is no sure-fire way to tell if you are a good person. No one point can be definitive. But you can definitely look at a combination of factors to determine the possibility of that age-old question. The only thing you can do is to constantly work on improving yourself. Invest time and effort into becoming a better person and never stop striving for growth in your character.

Chapter 27:
Stay Focused

A razor sharp focus is required to bridge the gap
between our vision and our current circumstances.
Stay focused on the vision we want,
despite the current reality.
It's challenging to believe you will be rich when you are poor,
healthy if you are sick,
but it is necessary to achieve that vision.

Focus on the desired result.
Focus on the next step towards that goal.
Without focus on these elements there can be no success.
Stay focused on the positive elements,
solutions over problems.

The expected reward over the fear, loss and pain along the way.
What we focus on will become.
Therefore we have to maintain our eyes on the prize.

Be results driven.
Always focus on bringing that result closer.
Focus on what your grateful for.
Gratefulness brings more of that into your life.

Focus on problems on the other hand brings more problems.

If we focus on a big goal today,
we might not be ready yet,
but we will become ready on the way.

Commit to the necessary changes you know you need.
Get ourselves ready for that goal.
So many never act simply because they don't know how.
They don't feel ready.
We can achieve nearly anything if we focus on it.

Think carefully about what you focus on.
It is critical to both your success and failure.
Know exactly what you want.
See the odds of a successful happy life increase by unfathomable amounts.

How can we be happy and successful if we never define what that is?
It's not about what you are, or what you were in the past.
It is all about what you are becoming and want to become.

We cannot let circumstances or the world decide that.
We must use our free will and decide who and what we will become and focus fully on that.
Wishing, succumbing to the days whim, will never bring lasting success.
Success requires serious commitment and focus on that outcome.

Exude a fanatical level of focus.
Be exuberated in the pursuit of success.

The most successful often focus on work for over 100 hours per week.
They give up most social interaction and even sleep to make that dream happen.
They do not find this hard or stressful because they are pursuing something they enjoy.

Focus on something you enjoy.
Stop spending your time and energy on a job that you hate.
Work in an area you enjoy.
It makes focusing and achieving success easier.

Keep in mind that your time is limited.
Is what you're doing right now moving you towards your goal?
If not stop.

It is crucial that you enjoy your journey.
Start planning some leisure time into your days.
The goal is to remain balanced while you stick to your schedule.

If you focus on nothing, you will receive nothing.
If you do nothing, you will become nothing.

Your focus is everything.

Get specific with your focus to steer your ships in the direction of the solid fertile land you desire.
Aim higher as you focus on bigger and better things.

Why focus on plan b if you believe in plan a?
Why not give all your focus to that?

Stay focused on the best result regardless of the perceived situation.
The world is pliable.
It will mould and change around you based on your thoughts and what you focus on.
Your free will means you are free to focus on what you want and ignore what you don't.

Focus on a future of greatness.
A future where you are healthy, happy, and wealthy.
See the limits as imaginary and watch them break down before you.
Understand that you are powerful and what you think matters in your life.

Become who you want to be,
Not who others think you should be.
This shift is one of the quickest roads to happiness.

When you focus on what you love,
You draw more of it into our lives.
You will become happier.

You must focus on a future that makes you and your family happy.

You must stay steadfast with an unwavering faith and focus on that result.

Because with faith and focus anything is possible.

Chapter 28: How To Start Working Immediately

"There is only one way for me to motivate myself to work hard: I don't think about it as hard work. I think about it as part of making myself into who I want to be. Once I've chosen to do something, I try not to think so much about how difficult or frustrating or impossible that might be; I just think about how good it must feel to be that or how proud I might be to have done that. Make hard look easy." - Marie Stein.

Motivation is somewhat elusive. Some days you feel it naturally, other days you don't, no matter how hard you try. You stare at your laptop screen or your essay at the desk, willing yourself to type or write; instead, you find yourself simply going through the motions, not caring about the work that you're producing. You're totally uninspired, and you don't know how to make yourself feel otherwise. You find yourself being dissatisfied, discouraged, frustrated, or disappointed to get your hands on those long-awaited tasks. While hoping for things to change and make our lives better overnight magically, we waste so much of our precious time. Sorry to burst your bubble, but things just don't happen like that. You have to push yourself off that couch, turn off the phone, switch off Netflix and make it happen. There's no need to seek anyone's permission or blessings to start your work.

The world doesn't care about how tired you are. Or, if you're feeling depressed or anxious, stop feeling sorry for yourself while you're at it. It doesn't matter one bit. We all face obstacles and challenges and struggles throughout our days, but how we deal with those obstacles and difficulties defines us and our successes in life. As James Clear once said, "Professionals stick to the schedule, amateurs let life get in the way. Professionals know what is important to them and work towards it with purpose; amateurs get pulled off course by the urgencies of life."

Take a deep breath. Brew in your favorite coffee. Eat something healthy. Take a shower, take a walk, talk to someone who lifts your energy, turn off your socials, and when you're done with all of them, set your mind straight and start working immediately. Think about the knowledge, the skill, the experience that you'll gain from working. Procrastination might feel good but imagine how amazing it will feel when you'll finally get your tasks, your work done. Don't leave anything for tomorrow. Start doing it today. We don't know what tomorrow might bring for us. If we will be able even to wake up and breathe. We don't know it for sure. So, start hustling today. You just need that activation energy to start your chain of events.

Start scheduling your work on your calendar and actually follow it. We may feel like we have plenty of time to get things done. Hence, we tend to ignore our work and take it easy. But to tell you the truth, time flickers by in seconds. Before you know it, you're already a week behind your deadline, and you still haven't started working yet. Keep reminding yourself as to why you need to do this work done. Define your goals and get them into action. Create a clear and compelling vision of your work. You only achieve what you see. Break your work into small, manageable tasks so you stay motivated throughout your work procedure. Get yourself organized. Unclutter your mind. Starve your distractions. Create that perfect environment so you can keep up with your work until you're done. Please choose to be successful and then stick to it.

You may feel like you're fatigued, or your mind will stop producing ideas and creativity after a while. But that's completely fine. Take a break. Set a timer for five minutes. Force yourself to work on the thing for five minutes, and after those five minutes, it won't feel too bad to keep going. Make a habit of doing the small tasks first, so they get out of the way, and you can harness your energy to tackle the more significant projects.

Reward yourself every time you complete your work. This will boost your confidence and will give you the strength to continue with your remaining tasks. Don't let your personal and professional responsibilities overwhelm you. Help yourself stay focused by keeping in mind that you're accountable for your own actions. Brian Roemmele, the Quora user, encourages people to own every moment, "You are in full control of this power. In your hands, you can build the tallest building and, in your hands, you can destroy the tallest buildings."

Start surrounding yourself with people who are an optimist and works hard. The saying goes, you're the average of the five people you hang out with the most. So, make sure you surround yourself with people who push you to succeed.

No matter how uninspired or de-motivating it may seem, you have to take that first step and start working. Whether it's a skill that you're learning, a language that you want to know, a dance step that you wish to perfect, a business idea that you want to implement, an instrument that you want to master, or simply doing the work for anyone else, you should do it immediately. Don't wait for the next minute, the next hour, the next day, or the following week; start doing your stuff. No one else is going to do your work for you, nor it's going to be completed by itself. Only you have the power to get on with it and get it done. Get your weak spots fixed. In the end, celebrate your achievements whether it's small or big. Imagine the relief of not having that task up on your plate anymore. Visualize yourself succeeding. It can help you stay to stay focused and motivated and get your work done. Even the worst tasks won't feel painful, but instead, they'll feel like a part of achieving something big.

Remember, motivation starts within. Find it, keep it and make it work wonders for you.

Chapter 29:
How to Love Yourself First

It's so easy to tell someone "Love yourself" and much more difficult to describe *how* to do it. Learn and practice these six steps to gradually start loving yourself more every day:

Step 1: Be willing to feel pain and take responsibility for your feelings.

Step 1 is mindfully following your breath to become present in your body and embrace all of your feelings. It's about moving toward your feelings rather than running away from them with various forms of self-abandonment, such as staying focused in your head, judging yourself, turning to addictions to numb out, etc. All feelings are informational.

Step 2: Move into the intent to learn.

Commit to learning about your emotions, even the ones that may be causing you pain, so that you can move into taking loving action.

Step 3: Learn about your false beliefs.

Step 3 is a deep and compassionate process of exploration—learning about your beliefs and behavior and what is happening with a person or situation that may be causing your pain. Ask your feeling self, your inner child: "What am I thinking or doing that's causing the painful feelings of anxiety, depression, guilt, shame, jealousy, anger, loneliness, or emptiness?" Allow the answer to come from inside, from your intuition and feelings.

Once you understand what you're thinking or doing that's causing these feelings, ask your ego about the fears and false beliefs leading to the self-abandoning thoughts and actions.

Step 4: Start a dialogue with your higher self.

It's not as hard to connect with your higher guidance as you may think. The key is to be open to learning about loving yourself. The answers may come immediately or over time. They may come in words or images or dreams. When your heart is open to learning, the answers will come.

Step 5: Take loving action.

Sometimes people think of "loving myself" as a feeling to be conjured up. A good way to look at loving yourself is by emphasizing the action: "What can I *do* to love myself?" rather than "How can I *feel* love for myself?"

By this point, you've already opened up to your pain, moved into learning, started a dialogue with your feelings, and tapped into your spiritual guidance. Step 5 involves taking one of the loving actions you identified in Step 4. However small they may seem at first, over time, these actions add up.

Step 6: Evaluate your action and begin again as needed.

Once you take the loving action, check in to see if your pain, anger, and shame are getting healed. If not, you go back through the steps until you discover the truth and loving actions that bring you peace, joy, and a deep sense of intrinsic worth.

Over time, you will discover that loving yourself improves everything in your life—your relationships, health and well-being, ability to manifest your dreams, and self-esteem. Loving and connecting with yourself is the key to loving and connecting with others and creating loving relationships. Loving yourself is the key to creating a passionate, fulfilled, and joyful life.

Chapter 30:

Why You're Demotivated By A Values Conflict

Every human being, in fact, every organism in this universe is different from even the same member of their species. Every one of us has different traits, likes, dislikes, colors, smells, interests so it's natural to have a difference of opinion.

It's natural to have a different point of view. It's natural and normal to have a different way of understanding. And it's definitely normal for someone else to disagree with your ways of dealing with things.

Most of us don't want to see someone disagreeing with us because we have this tricky little fellow inside of us that we call EGO.

Our ego makes us feel disappointed when we see or hear someone doing or saying something better than us. We cannot let go of the fact that someone might be right or that someone might be Okay with being wrong and we can't do a single thing about it.

This conflict of values occurs within ourselves as well. We want to do one thing but we cannot leave the other thing as well. We want to have something but we cannot keep it just because we don't have the resources to maintain them.

This feeling of 'want to have but cannot have' makes us susceptible to feelings of incompleteness ultimately making us depressed. The reality of life is that you can't always get what you want. But that doesn't make it a good enough reason to give up on your dreams or stop thinking about other things too.

Life has a lot to offer to us. So what if you can't have this one thing you wanted the most. Maybe it wasn't meant for you in the first place. Nature has a way of giving you blessings even when you feel like you have nothing.

Let's say you want something but your mind tells you that you can't have it. So what you should do is to find alternative ways to go around your original process of achieving that thing and wait for new results. What you should do is to give up on the idea altogether just because you have a conflict within your personality.

You cannot let this conflict that is building within you get a hold of you. Clear your mind, remove all doubts, get rid of all your fears of failure or rejection, and start working from a new angle with a new perspective. Set new goals and new gains from the same thing you wanted the first time. This time you might get it just because you already thought you had nothing to lose.

This feeling of 'No Regret' will eventually help you get over any situation you ever come across after a fight with your inner self. This feeling can help you flourish in any environment no matter what other people say or do behind your back.

Nothing can bring you peace but yourself. Nothing holds you back but your other half within you.

Chapter 31:
Why Are You Working So Hard

Your why,

your reason to get up in the morning,

the reason you act,

really is everything - for without it, there could be nothing.

Your why is the partner of your what,

that is what you want to achieve, your ultimate goal.

Your why will be what pushes you through the hard times on the path to your dreams.

It may be your children or a burning desire to help those less fortunate,

whatever the reason may be,

it is important to keep that in mind when faced with troubles or distractions.

Knowing what you want to do, and why you are doing it,

is of imperative importance for your life.

The tragedy is that most people are aiming for nothing.

They couldn't tell you why they are working in a certain field even if they tried.

Apart from the obvious financial payment,

They have no clue why they are there.

Is financial survival alone really a good motive to act?
Or would financial prosperity be guaranteed if you pursued greater personal preference?
Whatever your ambitions or preference in life,
make sure your why is important enough to you to guarantee your persistence.

Sometimes when pursuing a burning desire,
we can become distracted from the reason we are working.

Your why should be reflected in everything you do.
Once you convince yourself that your reason is important enough, you will not stop.
Despite the hardships, despite the fear, despite the loss and pain.
As long as you maintain a steady path of faith and resilience,
your work will soon start to pay off.
A light will protrude from the darkness and the illusionary troubles sent to test your faith will disappear as if they were never here.

Your why must be strong.
Your what must be as clear as the day is to you now.
And your faith must be eternal and unwavering.
Only then will the doors be opened to you.
This dream can be real, and will be.

When it is clear in the mind with faith, the world will move to show you the way.

The way will be revealed piece by piece, requiring you to take action and do the required work to bring your dream into reality.

Your why is so incredibly important.
The bigger your why, the greater the urgency, and the quicker your action will be.

Take the leap of faith.
Do what you didn't even know you could.
Never mind anyone else.
Taking the unknown path.
Perhaps against the advice of your family and friend,
But you know what your heart wants.

You know that even though the path will be dangerous, the reward will be tremendous.
The risks of not never finding out is too great.
The risk of never knowing if you could have done better is unfathomable.
You can always do better, and you must.

Knowing what is best for you may prove to be the most important thing for you.
How you feel about the work you are doing,
How you feel about the life you are living,
And how do you make the most of the time you have on this earth.
These may prove far more important than financial reward could ever do for you.

Aim to strike a balance.

A balance between working on what you are passionate about and building a wealthy financial life.

If your why and will are strong enough,

Success is all but guaranteed for you – no second guesses needed.

Aim for the sky,

However high you make it,

you will have proven you can indeed fly.

Chapter 32: Don't Make Life Harder Than It Needs To Be

Today we're going to talk about a topic that I hope will inspire you to make better decisions and to take things more lightly. As we go through this journey of life together, and as we get older, we soon find ourselves with more challenges that we need to face, more problems that we need to solve, and more responsibilities that we need to take on as an adult. In each phase of life, the bar gets set higher for us. When we are young, our troubles mostly revolve around school and education. For most of us we don't have to worry much about making money or trying to provide for a family, although I know that some of you who come from lesser well off families might have had to start doing a lot earlier. And to you i commend you greatly. For the rest of us we deal with problems with early teenage dating, body image, puberty, grades, and so on. It is only until we graduate from university do we face the harsh reality of the real world. Of being a working adult. It is only then are we really forced to grow up. To face nasty colleagues, bosses, customers, you name it. And that is only just the beginning.

Life starts to get more complicated for many of us when we start to realise that we have to manage our own finances now. When our parents stop giving us money and that we only have ourselves to rely on to survive. Suddenly reality hits us like a truck. We realise that making our own money becomes our primary focus and that we may not have much else to rely on. We take on loans, mortgages, credit card debts, and it seems to never really end. For many of us, we may end up in a rat race that we can't get out of because of the payments and loans that we have already ended up committing to. The things we buy have a direct impact on the obligations that have to maintain.

Next we have to worry about finding a partner, marriage, starting a family, buying a house, providing for your kids, setting aside money for their growth, college fund, the list goes on and on.

Do you feel overwhelmed with this summary of the first maybe one-third of your life? The reality is that that is probably the exact time line that most of us will eventually go through. The next phase of life requires us to keep up the payments, to go to our jobs, to keep making that dough to sustain our family. We may have to also make enough money to pay for tuition fees, holidays, gifts, payments to parents, and whatever other commitments that we might have. And this might go on until we reach 60, when two-thirds of our lives are already behind us.

Life as you can see, without any external help, is already complicated enough. If you didn't already know by now, life isn't easy. Life is full of challenges, obligations, obstacles, commitments, and this is without any unforeseen events that might happen... Medical or family wise.

With all this in mind, why do we want to make life harder than it already is?

Every additional decision that you make on top of this list will only add to your burden, if it is not the right one, and every person that you add into your life that is negative will only bring the experience much less enjoyable.

To make life easier for you and your soul, I recommend that you choose each step wisely. Choose carefully the partner that you intend to spend your life with, choose wisely the people that you choose to spend your time with, choose wisely the food that you put in your body, and choose wisely the life that you wish to lead.

Be absolutely clear on the vision that you have for your life because it ain't easy.

Another thing to make your life much less complicated is to put less pressure on yourself. I believe that you don't need to start comparing your life with others because everyone is on their own journey. Don't chase the fancy houses and cars that your friends have just because they have them. Everyone is different and everyone's priorities might be different as well. They might pride having a luxury car over spending on other areas of life, which might differ from the interests that you might have. Comparison will only most certainly lead you to chase a life that you might not even want to attain. And you might lose your sleep and mind trying to match up to your peers. Focus on yourself instead and on exactly what you want out of life and it will definitely be enough.

I challenge each and everyone of you to have a clear set of priorities for yourself. And once you have done so and are working towards those goals, be contented about it. Don't change the goalpost just because your friends say you must, or because you are jealous of what they have. Be satisfied in your own path and life will reward you with happiness as well.

Chapter 33:
6 Ways To Get Full Attention From People Around You

The long-term success of someone's life depends on getting the attention of others. Those others can include your teammates, your boss, your life partner, your clients, etc. But how? A person may ask. You cannot get promoted without getting your boss's attention, and your work cannot get appreciated by your teammates without awareness. To lead a healthy personal life, one may need to give attention to and from one's life partner, and of course, without the attention of your clients, how will your business survive?

Fortunately, there is plenty of research on how a human brain works and how it can focus on something. A lot of people have been researching about gaining people's attention for a long time now.

By some researchers, attention has been considered the "most important currency anybody can give you," although attention does make a person feel loved, it also gains your success. Fame can even come through negative attention, but it comes with hate as its price, whereas true and long-term success comes from positive attention. Here are six ways to get full attention from people around you.

1. **Stand In A Central Position**

When you are at a social gathering or a party, place yourself in a central position. Try to appear more friendly to new people, invite them over to your group, this way people will like you more. When you speak, they will pay attention—standing in a prominent place where everybody can see and talk to you easily will gain you more alert. Be being friendly to new individuals, and you will feel connected to others. Just be confident the whole time, and try to blend well with others and stand in a prominent place; this way, you will get more attention.

2. **Leave Some Mystery!**

Do you know what Zeigarnik Effect is? This effect suggests that the human brain tends to remember those things more, which is incomplete, as the question in their brain arises how? Where? And what?

This kind of technique is often used by professionals in business meetings, audience-oriented presentations. However, you can also use it in your daily life. When you introduce yourself to someone, don't just spill everything about yourself right away. Give the tiniest bit of pieces of information about something interesting, don't give the details just yet; wait for someone to ask for the details. And someone will surely ask, and you will get the desired attention.

3. **Use Body Language**

Most of us know how to communicate verbally, but do you know how to communicate non-verbally? Because non-verbal communication is as important as verbal communication. Maintain positive body language, and if you sit back slouched and give some closed-off vibes, it is less likely that you would catch someone's attention. To see some attention, you need to bring more positivity in your conversation and your body language. Don't cross your arms and legs when talking to someone; face them with an open posture and stand with confidence. Don't avoid eye contact but don't overdo it; try to maintain eye contact with everyone around you for a while. This will show your confidence and also builds a connection with others. Be relaxed confidently. Smiling while talking to someone indicates your friendliness and makes them feel welcome; this way, they feel comfortable and give you their undivided attention, but everybody would avoid talking to you if you look moody.

4. **Leave An Impression**

It is the subconscious habit of a human being to think more about the people who left a good impression on them, try to engage their senses like touch, hear, or vision. Who doesn't like fashion nowadays? Try to wear something fashionable and decent, the kind of outfit that will likely leave a good impression on others. You can also wear something that has a different color or a twist to it. Speak confidently and in a clear voice.

You can also put on a lovely perfume, cologne; try not to go overboard with this as nobody likes too much smell even if it is good.

5. **Having A Hype Team**

Having a hype team can easily capture a lot of attention; when you are in a not so formal setting, bring along your friends, surely they will be more than happy to excite you up. When you talk about your achievements among other people, it may seem to some that you are simply bragging. Still, when someone else talks about your accomplishments, it increases the interest of other people in you and gains you some positive attention.

6. **Find A Way To Sell Yourself Without Bragging**

A hype team is not always an option, but selling yourself without bragging is also something that needs to be done. What you don't need to discuss is;

- Your bank balance
- The expensive things you own
- Your occupation
- Your achievement

Conclusion

Brag through storytelling, and everybody loves an inspiring story. A successful person with a humble background always gains some attention. Attention plays an essential role in our lives, and you need to put a bit of effort into gaining it.

Chapter 34:
7 Ways On How To Expect Change For The Better In Your Life

The quicker you accept the fact that change is inevitable and can't be avoided, the better off you will be. The change could be better or worse; if you want it to be the former, you need to take complete control of your life. As life moves on, it's logical that the more transition and change you go through, the more opportunity you will have to perceive the patterns of your life, whether you will be able to handle the change or not, or how you can successfully negotiate and navigate these necessary transitions. We can do many things to turn our lives around; we can adopt habits and ideologies that will make us successful, but more importantly, happy. Now, you know yourself well enough to know what you want, what you realistically can do, and ideally, how you can accomplish those ideas and plans. Here are some ways to expect change for the better in your life.

1. **Find Meaning and Purpose**

Finding meaning in your life is easier said than done. You need to understand that knowing one's specific purpose takes more time than one can imagine. Life does not always go according to our plan; there are loads of unexpected changes that we have to deal with on our way. Therefore, it is essential to understand the difference between goals and purposes; we often confuse these two. For example, you might think that your purpose is to become a famous athlete or scientist or even the president. However, these are merely your goals and not your purpose. Your purpose should be broader and more open than your ambitions or passions. It must positively impact the world or even be a key to your happiness and love.

2. Love and Respect Yourself

How can you expect to gain the respect and love of people when you can't even do that for yourself? To bring a positive evolution in your life, you need to build your self-confidence and self-esteem, which can only be achieved by working hard on yourself and taking action. Whether you face rejections or failures, accepting all the negativity and loving yourself regardless will help you move on more quickly. Putting yourself down and clinging to regrets will get you nowhere. As long as you love yourself and are satisfied with yourself, the opinions of others shouldn't matter to you.

3. Stop Making Excuses

This is a rule that you should embody in your soul; if you want to achieve something and bring positive change in your life, then you should stop lying to yourself. Understand that your time is limited, and the excuses you make will only waste it. Every explanation for failure is ultimately an excuse, and they do nothing but bring you down. Life isn't as easy as we see in the movies. Success and happiness can't be achieved in the blink of an eye. There will be many obstacles, and life will throw some serious curveballs at you. But what matters, in the end, is how we keep moving forward despite it all. Instead of making excuses and lying to ourselves for our failures, we should keep working hard.

4. Develop The Habit of Positive Thinking

It is said to believe that positive thoughts and confidence bring positive changes in our life. Sure, only thinking about it won't lead you to success, but it will motivate you and help you to give your absolute best. The law of attraction is proved to be somewhat true to many people. Therefore, we should try to be more optimistic and envision ourselves achieving our goals and working hard towards them. We should be in a positive mindset all the time; even if something negative happens to us, we should focus on the good more.

5. Develop A Productive Routine

Having a productive routine is essential for a successful life; it is critical to manage your time wisely and eventually turn all the positive things into your habits. Start with smaller tasks, like making your bed after getting up. This can actually give you positive reinforcement to start your day and eventually lead to a happy and productive day.

6. Set Goals For Yourself

You need to set some goals if you want to achieve anything worthwhile in your life. These goals are what keeps you motivated and helps you to stay on track. Set both short-term as well as long-term goals and work hard towards achieving them. Remember, your goals can change along the way; you have to be flexible about it and focus on giving your best effort in their pursuit.

7. Live A Healthy Lifestyle

If your physical health is good, your mental health will be good, and vice versa. Adopting a healthier lifestyle can bring positive changes in your physical as well as mental health. It can help you turn your life around. It is essential to take care of our diet and make sure to exercise regularly. Good health is vital for a happy and content life.

Conclusion

To sum it up, by following the above tips, you will have a tremendously positive result. You will be able to change your life for the better.

www.ingramcontent.com/pod-product-compliance
Lightning Source LLC
LaVergne TN
LVHW010346070526
838199LV00065B/5797